May

Book recommended
by my friend Allen
Hickinger

STRENGTH TO
STRENGTH

STRENGTH TO STRENGTH

Meditations for
Spiritual Direction

ROB DES COTES

IMAGO DEI PUBLISHING

Imago Dei Publishing
19353-16th Avenue
Surrey, BC V3S 9V2 Canada
www.imagodeicommunity.ca

Unless otherwise noted, all Scripture quotations are from the
HOLY BIBLE, NEW INTERNATIONAL VERSION
copyright © 1973, 1978, 1984 by the International Bible Society

Cover design by Mark Des Cotes and Rob Des Cotes

Library and Archives Canada Cataloguing in Publication

Des Cotes, Rob, 1954-, author
Strength to Strength : meditations for spiritual direction
/ Rob Des Cotes.

ISBN 978-0-9920592-4-8 (paperback)

1. Spiritual life–Christianity–Meditations. I. Title.

BV4501.3.D485 2015   248.4   C2015-907566-1

CONTENTS

INTRODUCTION

It has always intrigued me how the saints from the past, though separated from one another by time and geography, nevertheless seem to be expressing the same experience when they describe what they learn about God and themselves through prayer. Most of them did not have access to each other's writings, but in the varied and subjective accounts of their encounters with God they all seem to be describing a similar landscape of the spiritual journey. Like a multi-faceted diamond their writings celebrate the many ways God has given us to express our relationship with Him.

This fact gives me hope that our individual path of prayer is not simply the product of our personal imagination, but that it represents just one more of the many facets of this diamond—a jewel that is both highly subjective as well as objectively true for all. Though we experience prayer in a most personal way we discover, as we articulate this experience to others, that what is most profoundly true for us is also true for them.

As we have discovered in our various Imago Dei groups there is fertile ground for fellowship that can be cultivated around the subject of prayer because of this simple fact—that what is most personal in our own experience of God also resonates deeply with the experiences of others. I believe this has always been the God-given basis for apprenticeship by which we learn from one another how to navigate well our own paths. And it is this encouragement that I wish to bring to others in what I write.

I have a quote in my office from St. Augustine that is related to this fact. I read it often as it articulates well my vocation and expresses the hope I have that what I learn about myself and God through prayer might also be of encouragement to others. With regards to his prayer life and its relationship to his writing Augustine says, "I wish to do this truth before you alone by praising you, and before a multitude of witnesses by writing of you." Spiritual truth, we discover, is not something we learn primarily through books, but more from our first-hand explorations of the creature's relationship with God. That which God teaches us about our own path then becomes the basis from which we offer encouragement to others. Together we learn to navigate this mysterious and objective landscape of prayer.

In the spirit of Augustine, these meditations are my way of responding to Jesus' greatest commandment—to love God and neighbour. They are like travelogues, documentations of things I have learned either through study or in my own reconnaissance in prayer that I hope might be of encouragement to others.

As with our three previous books, the meditations that follow were originally written as curriculum for our various Imago Dei groups as well as for individuals from around the world who subscribe to our weekly newsletter. The meditations that we send out each week also include discussion questions and suggestions for prayer response. If you would like to follow such a curriculum either on your own or with others, similar meditations can be found on our website under "Study Guides for ID Groups," or you can subscribe directly to these through our website.

As these meditations were originally sent out weekly, people had time to reflect on them over the course of a few days, and perhaps opportunity to discuss them with others. With this in mind I would suggest a certain pace in how you approach this book, especially to those who might otherwise read it in an hour and then move on to your next book (pastors, do take note).

Consider approaching each meditation as an icon—an image or a room one enters in order to meditate on one particular aspect of the spiritual life. Read them slowly, perhaps no more than one a day. Each meditation stands alone. Some of them are complex and perhaps need more time to digest and to let God interact with you in how they apply to your life. They are meant to simply prompt a dialogue within yourself or with others. Let them do so over the course of a few days as needed.

Of course, if you're like me, you will likely not heed any of these suggestions. That's ok too. You can always go back and do so on a second reading. Either way, my hope and prayer is that these meditations will serve to fan the flame of your desire for God and, in so doing, will dispose you more fully to bear the fruit of who you are becoming in Christ.

Rob Des Cotes
Loyola House
Guelph, Ontario
May, 2015

MEDITATIONS

1

And a highway will be there; it will be called the Way of
Holiness; it will be for those who walk on that Way.

Imagine a multitude of people walking along a raised path in the wilderness. They are crowded together, having to move carefully as there are ditches on either side of the highway. Most of the people seem to be walking resolutely towards some destination. You notice a marked difference though between those at the front of the line and those at the end, who are just beginning to join the throng. A significant transformation has taken place in the souls of those who have travelled longer on this path. It becomes evident, in light of this conversion, that the destination of this journey is not necessarily to a place but to an increasing state of freedom— a freedom associated with holiness.

Those at the front of the line seem to shine with a winsome glow that inspires and motivates the people behind them. Every now and then, those behind catch a glimpse of the virtue that the saints ahead of them are enjoying, causing a noticeable ripple of enthusiasm through the crowd. But regardless where people are positioned on this path, they seem satisfied and grateful to be there. The motivation that those ahead of them provide is not so much one of envy but one of anticipation that serves to quicken their step.

You notice, as well, that there are people wandering in the fields and rocky areas on either side of the raised highway, some alone and others in small groups. These people seem lost and oblivious to the parade that is passing right beside them. But you also notice some who are walking among them with much more of a sense of purpose. They are those who have temporarily sacrificed their place on the highway in order to go search for these lost souls. You watch as one of them approaches a group of wanderers and begins speaking to them. You can tell by the way she keeps pointing towards the highway that she is inviting them to come and join her in the journey. Some do, but many don't. Instead, they keep wandering in the field, their eyes looking far into the distance for whatever they are searching for.

There is a high hill nearby, off to the side of the road. You leave the crowd for a while to climb it, and you can now see the whole multitude at a glance. You notice that there is a bulge of people in the middle of the throng while the numbers seem to thin out at both the front and rear of the line. The ones in the middle are carrying items with them that will serve the whole community on their journey—tents, food, water, as well as musical instruments, books for teaching, liturgical vestments and other articles that express something of their common destination. Every night they set up their tents and serve the many people who gather for a common meal. It is an opportune time as well to share stories and to remind one another of the hope that inspires their trek.

At the rear of the line you see some people who are obviously new to this pilgrimage. Though they begin each day with enthusiasm they soon start complaining about tiredness, blisters and the heat of the noon-day sun. But there are others among them, people with the same glow as those in the front of the line. These are the ones who have purposely fallen back in the line, choosing instead to walk among the new pilgrims, encouraging them and reminding them of where they are going. They are keeping an eye out as well for stragglers who might get left behind.

Curiously, there is also something similar happening at the front of the line. You see people who had previously been glowing with the winsome radiance of purpose who are now sitting down, seemingly dejected on the side of the road. Their glow has faded as they seem confused about their way, disheartened by the challenges that the process of conversion continues to impose on them. Others from the front line leave the highway to sit with these people. They talk with them, gently offering encouragement to these discouraged souls. You notice the glow slowly return to these people and you are reminded of the similar effect Moses and Elijah had on Jesus when they ministered to Him at the time of His transfiguration.

As you strain to see how far the front line extends you are startled by what you notice. The people at the very front seem to be mysteriously disappearing. Their souls, which were getting brighter and brighter with each step, are now becoming increasingly transparent so that they blend into the bright light of the sun. They are becoming one with the light that has been leading them this whole journey so that they seem to disappear as they reflect the very holiness they have been seeking. The brightness of these souls naturally attracts the attention of the pilgrims behind them. Suddenly, these same people who just a moment ago were dragging their steps, are now throwing themselves forward, making a renewed offering of themselves to whatever lies ahead for them on this journey. They do this with such joy that it reminds you of your own deep desires for holiness—that you too have been called to walk on this highway.

You have been watching long enough. It is time for you to come down from the hill and rejoin this pilgrimage. You run back towards the highway. As the people on the path see you approaching they turn to welcome you. With a song of praise in your heart, you realize how blessed you are to be on this road. You too will soon reflect the light that now surrounds you. You thank God for this hope, and for the love you feel for all those who are walking with you on this pilgrimage. And with great joy, you go forth.

2

Where your treasure is, there your heart will be also.

Luke 12:34

In his book, *The Transforming Friendship*, Dr. James Houston offers a helpful definition of the spiritual life when he says that we are "in the discipline of exercising the heart of desire for God." This simple statement fully encompasses the motivation, the direction, as well as the ultimate destination of the spiritual life—that we are in a relationship of mutual desire with God. Like two lovers running to embrace each other, God draws near to us as we draw near to God (James 4:8).

To bring into focus the many longings of our heart so that they find expression in the foundational desire that underlies all our seeking is our spiritual direction. And the more intentional we are in participating with this underlying desire the more we will discover the living waters of God's highest vision for our humanity. In the merging of our own desires with God's we will find our lives abundantly expressed.

As we are weaned from the many alternatives that misdirect our yearnings for God we also discover a greater sense of unity in our lives. In the consolidation of our heart's longings we become more directly engaged with their true object. We also find, as our desires align with those of God, that our longings become fewer, but stronger. It is a slow process, but one that ultimately leads us from dissipation to an undivided heart.

A sustained desire for prayer is evidence of the extent to which our lives are given over to God. If we are self-oriented, our longing for God and our motivation to prayer will be quenched. But the more we abandon ourselves to God's desires, the more sustained we will be in our zeal. As Houston puts it,

> Self-confidence robs us of the incentive to pray as we should. But when all our significance, security, identity and future are in the hands of God, then prayer is bound to follow.

The spiritual life invites us to return to our Father's house. And the countless choices we make each day are what determine our direction, either towards or away from God. They reveal the truth of Jesus' teaching that "where your treasure is, there your heart will be also" (Luke 12:34).

> *Unless your soul is continually lifted up to God, your flesh will drag it down. Therefore, you must renew your determination for the spiritual life each day.*
>
> St. Frances de Sales

3

I do not concern myself with great matters
or things too wonderful for me.
But I have stilled and quieted my soul;
like a weaned child with its mother.

Psalm 131:1b-2a

M any Christians do not enjoy the full benefits of a life of faith. Though they believe in God, they do not necessarily live in the experience of faith that should accompany that belief. They may, for instance, accept the theology that God is with them, and yet, for the most part, they walk alone in their day. They may believe that Christ forgives their sins and yet they continue to suffer from guilt and shame. They may believe the Scriptures that teach us how God provides for us and yet they are often fearful for their security. They know that their future is in God's hands, and yet they fret because they are unable to discern that future for themselves.

For all who suffer from such lack of faith, Psalm 131 offers an effective prescription for change. It invites us to leave behind the anxieties of faithless belief, and to embrace the maturity of trust whereby we can rest more securely in God's good care. The Psalm contrasts the turmoil of an overly reasoned life with that of quiet faith. It encourages us to let go of the adult concerns of the one in favour of the child-like trust of the other. David' sentiment is of one who says to himself, "I have had enough of worrying about my life's direction. I am tired of dealing with the unknowability of matters too great for me. I am ready for plan B."

If, like David, you too are tired of trying to work out the Rubik's cube of your life, Psalm 131 offers another approach. Rather than obsess over that which, at best, can only be speculated, it invites you to quiet your heart and to entrust the unknowable aspects of your life to God. If we have faith that the unknowns are not unknown to God, we can rest more securely in the God-ordained mystery of our blind spots. This, as David suggests, is the trusting disposition of a weaned child.

The image of a weaned child represents a healthy detachment from the type of clinging that often keeps our relationship with God at an infant stage. A weaned child is one who is free of the primal fears of babyhood. It no longer suffers the separation anxiety common to toddlers who see their mothers solely in terms of security and provision. The child who is weaned is secure enough about his mother's care to not be anxious about losing her care. This more confident disposition of faith also represents a greater freedom for the mother as it gives her permission to be who she is, apart from the child's immediate sense of need.

Love gives freedom to the other person to be who they are, and it is a mark of mature spirituality when we trust God to love us according to God's own freedom. In confident faith we allow God to hold our future without the distrust implied by our anxieties over what we can't see. Weaned from the imperatives of our need-based relationship, we are now more able to live in the freedom of faith. And the more confident we are that the Lord holds our future, the less concerned we need be of where we are going.

When my spirit grows faint within me,
it is you who know my way.

Psalm 142:3

4

Go into your inner room, close your door and pray to your
Father who is in secret, and your Father who sees what is
done in secret will reward you.

Mat. 6:6 (NASB)

According to Henri Nouwen, the chief task of the contemplative is to learn how to enter, and remain, in the solitude of his/her own heart. Nouwen writes,

> We have to fashion our own closet where we can withdraw every day and dwell in the gentle healing presence of our Lord. Without such a place we will lose our own soul, even while preaching the gospels to others.

For the desert monks of the fourth and fifth centuries, the equivalent of the closet was the *kellion*, or cell, in which they lived their lives in isolation, and where they encountered the deeper truth of their relationship with

God. The cell was seen as a school, sufficient to teach us all we need for the spiritual life. There is a story of a young monk who came to Father Moses for spiritual advice. Rather than give him counsel, Father Moses simply told the monk to "Go to your cell and sit down, and the cell will teach you everything."

Anselm Gruen, a contemporary Benedictine monk and author of *Heaven Begins Within You,* speaks as well of the transformative and educative power of the cell of our own solitude. He affirms Father Moses' advice regarding the benefits of our "inner room" saying,

> If we stay in our cells something in us will be transformed; we will find order within ourselves. We will come face to face with all the inner chaos that surfaces in us. And we will learn how to not run away from it.

Prayer transforms us by opening the eyes of our heart to the actual truth of who we are, and therefore to the truth of God's actual relationship with us. For the early monks, encounter with oneself was the precondition for every authentic encounter with God. And *stabilitas*—the constancy of holding on, and staying with oneself—was the prerequisite for every kind of human and spiritual progress.

Our capacity to remain with our selves, in spite of all our impulses to flee, is perhaps the main discipline we learn from solitude. That is why the ancient fathers stressed the importance of holding out and not running away from solitude. Anselm Gruen writes,

> Remaining in one's cell, keeping to oneself, is the necessary condition for both spiritual progress and maturation as a human being. The tree must send down roots to be able to grow. Continual uprooting and transplanting only blocks its development. One cannot be a mature person without the courage to hold out and meet one's own truth head on.

We must resist the temptation to flee from prayer. If we stay in our cell, we will grow in our true sense of reality. We will no longer be fooled by pretensions, either about ourselves or our relationship with God. The prayerful acceptance of "what is" will heal us from our inordinate impatience with life—the very thing that keeps us in such a restless state. This is why desert wisdom often refers to the cell as an infirmary, a place where the sick can get better. Gruen adds,

It is a place of wholeness, a place for healing, because we sense God's loving and healing nearness there. But I can have this positive experience of the cell only if I stay there even when everything in me rebels against it, when I am full of unrest. Once I have overcome this first phase, then I can begin to experience the cell as heaven.

Jesus' invitation in John 15 is for us to simply "remain in His love." When we consider the many excuses we have for straying from this love we can see the importance of learning how to remain with God in the secret place of our heart. There, we will meet the truth head on. And there we will find the way that leads, beyond the illusions of impatience, to a growing acceptance of our real relationship with God.

5

God's kindness is intended to lead you to repentance.

Rom. 2:4

Everybody wants to change. It is one of the primary themes of our Christian hope—that change is not only possible, but that it is God-ordained and God-empowered. A sustained desire for change expresses the living hope that we can actually become the people we feel called to be. And our participation with such change is one of the more direct ways that we honour God—by submitting to the transforming action of His love in our lives.

Change, for any of us, begins with a deep and honest desire for renewal, which the Bible calls repentance. It is the spirit by which we recognize that what we are is less than we should be, and by which we welcome the transformation that God invites us to. One of the truths that motivates us in our desire to change is, of course, God's goodness. We recognize the gracious gift of salvation that God has given us through Jesus, and we respond by consecrating our lives out of love, worship, and gratitude for what He has done.

We are also motivated to change by a growing awareness of our need for healing. As we recognize the many ways we are trapped and hindered by habitual behaviours and addictions, we find ourselves desperately seeking alternatives. We come to God in the hope of being freed from whatever keeps us captive to life. Recognizing the disorder within, we welcome the ministry of the Great Physician in faith that He not only has the power, but also the desire to heal us. The confidence by which we embrace such faith is evidence of the Holy Spirit within us, actively drawing us to Jesus for healing.

Repentance, then, is ultimately an act of hope that lies at the heart of spiritual growth. We welcome with gratitude the desire for transformation that the Holy Spirit inspires in us, as well as the God-given faith that such change is actually possible for us. We marvel that this hope continually resurrects in us, and that we do not, more naturally, succumb to despair. We watch ourselves rise, again and again, in the assurance that "He who began a good work in us will carry it on to completion" (Phil. 1:6).

Because we believe in the promise of God, we confidently anticipate the gift of a transformed life. Through the same Spirit who empowers us to seek purity, we celebrate the realistic hope that change is not only possible, but inevitable as long as we remain attached to the vine of Christ.

6

Whoever does not love does not know God, because God is love.

1John 4:8

There are many people who are not sure if they've ever had a real experience of God in their lives. They hear others speak so confidently of God "moving" in them, prompting them to act, or even speaking to them, and it leaves them feeling that they have perhaps been overlooked by God. I suspect, though, that this represents more a question of vocabulary—the things we name as God in our lives—than actual evidence of God's absence.

The Orthodox theologian Paul Evdokimov says that, "God is nearer to us than we are to ourselves." But it is this very radical nearness that often makes it difficult to detect the subtlety of God's presence within us. We don't recognize God because He is so close to us. As Evdokimov writes,

> The way God moves within us is usually quite natural to us. So much so that it is easy to assume that these movements are our

own. When people first recognize God's "voice" within them they are often surprised at how familiar it is. They've always known this voice but they never knew it was God. It takes discernment to be able to distinguish God's movement within us from our own, but it can be done. And the more we recognize the subtle artistry of God, the more we will know what to watch for.

The apostle John offers what is perhaps one of the easiest ways of recognizing God's presence within us when he summarizes the fact that "God is love." He does not say that "God has love" but that "God is love." To know love, then, is to know God. The fact that "whoever does not love, does not know God," naturally implies the converse—that the one who does love, does know God. Rather than thinking of love then as something that originates solely from us, we can more accurately see it as a "theophany" of God that has visited our hearts, causing His presence to well up within us in relationship to whatever we feel love for.

We can also apply this same discernment to our experiences of peace and joy. Jesus, after all, identifies Himself often with experiences of peace and joy that He claims come directly from His initiative (Jn 14:27, Jn 15:11). Could these common experiences be the very occasions for communion with God that we seek? In times when we are graced with love, peace or joy, could we not presume this to be the felt evidence of the Holy Spirit's presence within us? That it is *because* God is near, and touching our hearts, that we feel such things?

Though not every experience of peace, joy and love necessarily comes from God, it is certainly true to say that such experiences are consistent with the character and the effects of God as revealed to us in Scripture. If God, then, is prepared to declare Himself to us in such ways, we should not hesitate to ask Him, "Lord, what are the experiences within me that I've been calling myself, that are really the initiatives of your Holy Spirit?" As we learn to objectify the many varied movements of spirit within us, we will increasingly recognize the subtle artistry of God's presence in our hearts.

7

I have set before you life and death, blessings and curses.
Now choose life.

Deut. 30:19

There are two very distinct ways by which people seem to come to God—I call them "the way of suffering," and "the way of delight." Scripture offers many examples where both these two paths of return are illustrated. Perhaps the most obvious ones are Jesus' parable of the prodigal son, and His parable of the precious pearl.

In the first parable, it is the desolation the prodigal son is experiencing that ultimately restores him to his right mind. The increasing pain of his predicament prompts him to finally say, "I must return to my father's house." This is the way of suffering. Unfortunately it is the one that most often awakens us to the remembrance of God. The prodigal's life has withered, and it is the increasing dissatisfaction he is experiencing that finally inspires him to seek God. Though not all our tribulations are of this nature, the Bible is pretty clear that suffering is one of the natural results of straying from the movement of God's will (see e.g. Deut. 28:15-68, Psalm 107, Lam. 1:8, 14, Matt. 7:26-27, John 15:6, 2Pet. 2:20-21).

The way of suffering is a *via negativa.* It leads us to God by a path of remorse. The *via positiva,* however, leads us by an opposite route. This is the way of desire—the path Jesus encourages us to take when, for instance, He compares the kingdom of God to a precious pearl. It is the pearl's great worth that inspires the positive motivation for our spiritual direction. Having tasted that the Lord is good, we now long for the deeper intimacy we know is possible for our lives.

The way of desire is the way of the pilgrim. People on this path recognize the value of the prize and now press on "to take hold of that for which Christ Jesus took hold of me" (Phil. 3:12) They know where they are going and are motivated by joy, anticipating not only where this path is leading them, but also who they are becoming by following it.

If the *via negativa* is a road paved in warnings, cautions and reprimands, the path of desire is blazed in vision, hope and promise. Both paths are effective. They each offer their own motivations for returning to God, but it is easy to imagine which one our Father would prefer us to take.

I have set before you life and death—therefore choose life. The person traveling on the way of desire has made a choice. Like the prodigal son, they have suffered enough and never want to stray from home again. The spiritual life, for them, is non-negotiable. Their delight—to remain in His love—is the prime motivation that now keeps them attached to the life of Christ, not only because of the safety He provides but, more importantly, because of the joy that lays before them.

8

I urge you, brothers and sisters, in view of God's mercy, to offer your bodies as a living sacrifice, holy and pleasing to God—this is your true and proper worship.

Rom 12:1

Contemplative prayer cultivates the more receptive side of our relationship with God, a side that most of us need to grow in. Through it we discover a new vocabulary of intimacy with God. Over the course of twenty minutes or an hour of silent prayer we also come to appreciate the transformation that takes place in us as the topic of this dialogue shifts from ourselves to God.

The first stage of our prayer is often an opportunity for us to talk to the Lord about our lives. Questions are usually the most appropriate way to dialogue at this stage. How am I doing Lord? What do you think of this or that in me? It is a time to also consider our relationship to people and circumstances. What about my friends Lord? What about so and so who is struggling right now? And what about that worrisome situation coming up Lord? We also find ourselves dialoguing with God about the inner movements of our lives. What about this deep desire that keeps welling up in me Lord? What relationship should I have to this movement? And what about those fears that keep coming back to me? Am I worrying for nothing?

In the midst of such prayers, we often sense the Lord interacting with us. Perhaps it is a fresh enthusiasm that comes to our hearts, or a gentle spirit of peace that suddenly wafts into our soul and we suspect this might be God, who is subtly communicating His presence to us.

Eventually, though, we find ourselves less concerned with details and more able to focus on the non-verbal communication we are enjoying in God. The environment of prayer has changed from an active dialogue with God to a more passive one. Our attention is now more on our relationship with the Divine than with ourselves or our circumstances.

As we alternate in and out of this more simplified prayer, we perhaps note the difference between the prayer of the mind and the prayer of the heart. We realize there is a choice to be made as to which will claim our focus. We sense an invitation from the Holy Spirit encouraging us to surrender to this call. And, like clay, we offer ourselves to Jesus for whatever He is doing in us. Our desire now is to place ourselves more completely in the Lord's hands, trusting our Creator with our lives.

For these few and precious moments, we are truly Christ's servants. At long last, our lives are no longer our own, but His. As living sacrifices, and out of love for our Maker, we more fully yield to His will. It is what Paul appropriately calls our "true and proper worship."

9

He will teach us his ways, so that we may walk in his paths.

Micah 4:2

Any of you who are parents will certainly remember the many stages your toddlers went through as they first learned to walk. You might especially recall the role you had in helping them. You'll remember standing behind your child, perhaps holding their hands above their heads as they took their first step. You'll remember as well when you started letting them find their own balance, all the while gently holding their hands in yours.

You'll also remember the next stage, when they first started toddling on their own. Perhaps you were walking alongside them, hands outstretched and ready to catch them when they fell. You were the invisible presence that accompanied them in their first fledgling steps. You'll also surely remember the giggles when your little one faltered and immediately found your hands securing them in their fall. It was like a game to them. Something about the risk thrilled them, and they especially loved discovering, over and over again, that you were nearby, ready to catch them when they fell.

The next stage was perhaps the most fun one—when your child was now able to take a few steps on their own without falling. Instead of standing behind them, you now placed yourself a few feet in front of them. As they stood holding onto a table or chair, you would call them to come to you, coaxing them to leave the security of whatever they were holding onto and hoping they would be attracted enough to you to overcome their fears and cross this divide that you had purposely created for them to bridge.

You remember perhaps the hesitation in their eyes, doubting whether they could do this or not. Reaching out, you tried to draw them to you and were thrilled when you saw your child finally take that first step. You watched them stumble towards you, their legs trying to catch up with the enthusiasm that was driving them forward. You weren't sure if they were going to make it. They weren't sure either. But somehow they did, even if the last step was a wild and ungracious tumble onto your lap. They made it! That's all that mattered.

These are precious memories that every parent who has encouraged their child's first steps will fondly remember. God too has similar memories of you in every new path He has encouraged you in. He too, remembers standing behind you, holding your hands above your head while you tried to walk. He too remembers your first solo steps, when He stayed especially close to you, ready to catch you the moment you fell. And He too, in so many ways, still stands before you, coaxing you to leave that table or chair that secures you. He calls you to cross the room and to bridge the divide that He has purposely created in order to teach you how to walk towards Him on your own. And we can be pretty certain that God too rejoices in the great satisfaction He sees in you every time you "make it."

10

The one who loves God is known by God.

1Cor. 8:3

The contemplative life is a pilgrimage that both begins and ends in love since love is not only the cause of our contemplation of God but also its goal. Love leads us to a right understanding of relationship with the Divine. As St. Thomas of Aquinas taught in his *Summa Theologica*, "It is by the burning of love that we arrive at the knowledge of Truth." Thomas Merton, in his book, *The Ascent to Truth,* also speaks of the movement of love through prayer. He writes,

> The experience of union with God is one that can only be met in love. Our understanding will never reach God as our love will. Only love can establish the vital contact in which we "touch" the very substance of God.

Through love we experience God in a more perfect way than we ever could through our intellect. Examining the love we have for God also puts us in direct relationship with the love God has for us. Merton writes of this intuition whereby we reflect upon our experience of love.

> The soul feels in itself an intense love for God, reflects on that love, and adds to this reflection the thought that it is also loved beyond measure by God Himself. Love itself then becomes the object of knowledge. It is our love that we end up contemplating.

Contemplation inspires love in us while, at the same time, God is recognized in the very experience of love that contemplation produces in us. That is why the goal of prayer is not for the perfection of the one who is praying. Rather it is fulfilled in the object of our contemplation—which is our love for God. Again Merton writes,

> Divine love transfigures the soul and makes it the medium in which God is known. The soul, touched and transfigured by the flame of God's immediate presence, is no longer the object of knowledge but the actual medium in which God is known. Hence God, intimately experienced, becomes the object of the soul's contemplation.

The apostle John tells us that "God *is* love" (1Jn 4:8). There is therefore no distinction between the love we feel for God and the presence of God by which we feel it. To love God, in other words, is to know God. And to love God is to be united with the essence of who God is. As Merton puts it,

> Since our souls are spiritual substances and since God is pure Spirit, there is nothing to prevent a union between ourselves and God. In making us love Him as He loves us, God is said to take the soul entirely to Himself and to give Himself entirely to the soul. When God does this there is no longer any practical or experiential

distinction between His activity and the activity of the soul united in the same perfect love.

The Lord invites us to a growing relationship of pure love. And it is our response to that love that ultimately confirms the accuracy of our knowledge of God. As St. Bernard de Clairvaux taught, "If we know God and do not love Him, what we know is not God." The vision of Christian maturity recognizes that the journey of prayer ends in the perfect love of God. Contemplative prayer, then, is best understood as simply a means to that end.

> *The ultimate perfection of the contemplative life consists in the fact that God's truth is not only understood but is also loved.*
>
> St. Thomas of Aquinas

11

There is no fear in love, but perfect love casts out fear because fear has to do with punishment.

1Jn. 4:18

Love and fear are naturally at odds with each other. Fear causes us to withhold love. But, according to John's word, love can overcome our fears. In spite of the instinct that makes us want to protect ourselves as a first consideration, for the sake of love, we can learn to cast aside our fears.

Fear is for the self; love is for the other. When I am dominated more by fear than by love, my attitude towards the world is egocentric (centered on self) rather than heterocentric (centered on others). Whereas love leads us in the direction of freedom and trust, fear is more about self-protection. When fear predominates I withdraw from the love of others and retreat into myself.

Because fear motivates defensive thinking and action it hinders the fostering of close relationship with others. As fear quickens my defenses I tend to respond by either withdrawing or by adopting an aggressive attitude towards the other person. Though its goal is to protect the self, the more I am governed by fear, and the more I think I must control the people and circumstances around me, the more helpless and vulnerable I feel about life. Preoccupied with the thought of protecting myself, I end up feeling more and more alone in the world.

All forms of community are bedeviled with fear, as is our relationship with God. In his book, Spiritual Direction and the Encounter with God, William Barry speaks of the fluctuating dynamics of fear—how we tend to go back and forth in repeated patterns of withdrawal and return to intimacy. Barry writes,

> The pattern of withdrawal and return characterizes all the relationships in our lives, including our relationship with God. The withdrawal shows itself in our resistance to God's offers of intimacy, and the return in the overcoming of this resistance. "Only perfect love casts out fear," and our peace lies in attaining that perfect love, or at least in moving toward it.

If our relationships are overly defined by fear we will experience an inordinate sense of aloneness in life. The very strategies we cultivate for self-protection will only serve to accentuate our fears and our sense of separateness. But if, by God's grace, we overcome this first instinct in order to exercise love as the catalyst for relationship we will find the perfecting of this love to be the most effective way to cast out our fears.

12

He has filled the hungry with good things.

Luke 1:53

In order to be filled with the fullness of Christ, we must first be emptied of that which already fills us. As Mother Teresa so plainly puts it,

> God cannot fill what is already full, He can fill only emptiness – deep poverty. We have to be completely empty to let God do what He wills so that we can receive Him fully in our life and let Him live His life in us.

To be open space for God is to imitate Christ, who "made Himself nothing" (Phil. 2:7). In the example of His own life, Jesus modeled the posture of self-emptying "kenosis" as the most perfect vehicle through which the Father's will might be expressed. Mother Teresa urges her sisters to follow the Lord in this same disposition saying,

> God has shown His greatness by using our nothingness. So let us
> always serve Him by remaining in our nothingness, so as to give
> God a free hand to use us without even consulting us.

Incarnate within us, Jesus continues the life He lived on earth—that of
complete submission to the Father's will. The Lord receives the offering of
our compliance and then draws us deeper into His own relationship to the
Father. Regarding the action of Jesus' kenosis, now continuing in us,
Mother Teresa writes,

> Jesus wants to relive His complete submission to His Father in you
> today. Allow Him to do so. Take away your eyes from your self
> and rejoice that you have nothing, that you are nothing, that you
> can do nothing.

Prayer helps us to be more given to God. But a life consecrated to the
will of God is always challenged by our propensity to act according to our
own volition. Recognizing this, Mother Teresa wisely asks her sisters to
pray for her, that she would not be tempted with self-reliance. Even when
struggling in the depths of spiritual darkness she writes,

> Pray for me that in this darkness I do not light my own light, nor
> fill this emptiness with my self. I want with my whole will only
> Jesus. Pray for me that He may use me to the full.

Such saints, over the centuries, have shown us how to live according to
the many paradoxes of the spiritual life—that to become more, we must
become less; that to be filled, we must become empty; that in order to gain,
we must first let go. Their obedience to such divine instincts, and the fruit
they have borne as a result of their own submission, give us confidence to
believe that those who offer themselves as space for God will find that space
gloriously filled.

> *Perfect faith is when we are nothing but space for God to be God*
> *in us.*
>
> Fr. Simon Tugwell

13

*My Word will not return to me empty, but will accomplish
what I desire and achieve the purpose for which I sent it.*

Isaiah 55:10-11

I am grateful for the insight of P.T. Forsyth regarding the glory of prayer that originates in heaven, finds its voice in us, and then returns to heaven. His way of understanding this movement of God inspires me every time I pray.

Forsyth sums up the whole intent of Jesus' Incarnation in one sentence when he writes, "the whole rhythm of Christ's soul is of the Godhead going out, and returning on itself." Jesus' life on earth is God's outreach whereby a net has been cast through which humanity is now being drawn back to God. Forsyth sees our prayer life as having its origin in this same initiative of God when he writes,

> The prayer that reaches heaven began there, when Christ went forth. It began when God turned to beseech us in Christ. The Spirit went out with the power and function in it to return with our soul.

God sends the word to us and it does not return empty. It carries us back to its source. And this action, of our returning to God, is most evident in our response of prayer. As Forsyth puts it,

> God's Spirit returns to Him who gave it; and returns not void, but bearing our souls with Him. The soul runs its true course back to God its Creator, who has placed on it the destiny of this return, and who leaves it no peace till it finds its goal in Him.

Through the articulation of our prayers, Jesus carries our hearts to the Father and it is Christ's continual intercession for us at the Father's throne that now resonates in our response. Forsyth elaborates on this,

> Our prayer is the answer to God's. The intercession of Christ in heaven is the continuity and consummation of His supreme work on earth. To share it is the meaning of praying in the Spirit. For it is Christ at prayer who lives in us, and we are conduits of the Eternal Intercession.

In our hearts the Holy Spirit echoes the prayer that Christ is presently making for us at the Father's throne. What might appear as our own meager attempt to reach out to God is, in fact, Jesus' intercession, expressed within us as the groaning of our spirits. There we experience the first utterances of a language that wells up in the impulse to pray, which Jesus then translates to the Father's ear as perfect prayer. Forsyth sees this movement as the consummation of Christ's work of salvation when he writes,

> All along, Christ is being formed in us as we pray; and our converse with God goes on to become an element of the discourse between the Father and the Son. In Christ's intercession for us, our prayer, broken, soiled, and feeble as it is, is caught up and made prayer indeed and power with God. His intercession prays for our very prayer, and atones for all that is lacking in it.

Thanks be to God that perfect prayer does not depend on us. We are swept up rather by the action of Christ's prayer, which gathers us as a perpetual thank-offering to the Father. God's word, which wells up in our hearts, is accomplishing all that He desired it to accomplish. And His most articulated desire has always been for our return.

14

Our citizenship is in heaven. And we eagerly await a Savior from there, the Lord Jesus Christ, who, by the power that enables him to bring everything under his control, will transform our lowly bodies so that they will be like his glorious body.

Phil. 3:20-21

The Holy Spirit is always inviting us to submit more perfectly, out of love, to the immediate will of God. This is the maturing of spiritual direction that ushers in the reign of Christ. It is how the Lord conquers each individual heart, gradually bringing into subjection every believer to Himself.

Madame Guyon, a 17th century spiritual director, served this same objective as she always encouraged in the lives of others a growing submission to Christ. Guyon understood her ministry in terms of labouring for the increase of Christ's reign on earth, beginning in the very hearts of those she counseled. To one of her directees, for instance, she wrote,

> Since Jesus Christ appeared on earth, there is a general belief that the kingdoms of this world will ultimately be subject to His dominion. But we may ask, who hastens His coming, by now yielding up his own heart to His entire control?

Christ's kingdom is established in the hearts of those who are disposed to give the Lord free reign in their lives. They bow to their King, prepared to do or to become whatever best serves their Master. Madam Guyon likens this quality of self-offering to the fluidity of water when she writes,

> When the soul is perfectly yielding, it loses all its own consistency in order to take, any moment, the shape that God gives it, as water takes all the form of the vases into which it is poured. Suppleness of soul, therefore, is of vital importance to its progress. It is the work of God to effect this.

God desires that His will be reflected in us, and the Holy Spirit invites and enables us to grow in the disposition of submissive trust that this requires. The increasing reign of Christ in our lives is simply an answer to the second petition of the Lord's Prayer, as applied to ourselves—"thy will be done in me as it is in heaven." As Madame Guyon teaches her directee, "When the divine Word operates in the soul, without any obstruction, the soul becomes what this Word wills it should become."

The loyal subjects of a King are those who place their lives most completely at the disposal of His good will. Choosing to remain submissive, they offer themselves in preparation and anticipation of their Lord's promptings. To those who long for the reign of Christ to be established in their lives Madame Guyon offers this counsel:

> Your only preparation is abandonment to God, and remaining quiet in his hands. Possess your soul in peace as much as possible; not by effort, but by ceasing from effort; by letting go of everything that troubles you. Be quiet, so that your heart may be settled. As we leave water to settle when agitated so will you have clarity according to the peace of God that is established in your soul.

Christ's reign, characterized by the tranquility, gentleness and strength of our Lord's own virtue, will reveal itself most evidently in the countenance of our lives. As His sovereignty increases within us, there will be that much more evidence of the effects of His Peace on earth.

Jesus, may all that is You flow into me
May Your body and blood be my food and drink
May Your passion and death be my strength and life.

from St. Ignatius' "Soul of Christ" prayer

15

He has set eternity in the hearts of men and women.

Eccl. 3:11

The idea that both the Sabbath and eternity share something of the same essence is an ancient one in Jewish theology where the Sabbath is welcomed each week as an anticipation of heaven. As one ancient tradition declares: "The world to come is characterized by the kind of holiness possessed by the Sabbath in this world, and the Sabbath possesses a holiness like that of the world to come."

The Sabbath then serves to remind us that we belong simultaneously to two worlds—to this world as well as the next. We are to long for the Sabbath in the same way we long for eternity, which is why Judaism tries to foster the vision of life as a weekly pilgrimage towards the seventh day. As the Jewish theologian Abraham Heschel states,

> All our life should be a pilgrimage to the seventh day. The thought and appreciation of what this day may bring to us should be ever present in our minds as inspiring our vision of eternity. For the Sabbath is the counterpoint to the active, temporal life.

Rabbi Solomon, in his 11th century commentary on the Talmud, speaks similarly of the relationship between our temporal observance of the Sabbath and our anticipation of heaven. He writes,

> Unless one learns how to relish the taste of Sabbath while still in this world, as an initiation in our appreciation of eternal life, one will be unable to anticipate with joy the taste of eternity for the world to come. Sad is the lot of anyone who arrives inexperienced and, when led to heaven, cannot perceive there the familiar beauty of the Sabbath.

As the Sabbath is part of God's inaugural act of creation, so is it a symbol of the final act of creation. This is why the writer of the book of Hebrews encourages us, in this life, to make every effort to enter the "Sabbath-rest" that still awaits the people of God (Heb. 4:9-10). In light of the eternity that the Sabbath foreshadows, we are to cultivate the art of anticipating, each week, the day God has deemed as holy. Let us creatively prepare ourselves to receive the blessing that the Lord has promised us on our day of rest. And, above all, let us learn to relish, while still in this world, the God-given delights of the eternal Sabbath that we await.

16

Are not two sparrows sold for a penny? Yet not one of them will fall to the ground outside your Father's care.

Mat. 10:29

When my son was two years old we used to play a game of trust where he would jump into my arms from the roof of our Volkswagen van. I was the one who called it a game of trust. He simply called it fun. I would lift him onto the roof of our van, stand back a few feet, and then invite him to jump off. Without a moment's hesitation he would leap into my arms. I would put him back on the van, take another step back and call him to jump again. And once more he would fly off the roof into my arms, laughing all the way. I remember doing this after church one Sunday and having a little crowd gather around to watch. It was quite a spectacle to see.

But I will always remember the last time we played this game together. As we had done so many times before I put my son on the roof and waited for him to jump to me. And then I saw it in his face. Whatever thought entered his mind, I knew that it had introduced to him the notion of fear. For the first time in his short life, he had entertained the possibility that I might not actually catch him. I could see the struggle between faith and doubt so evident in his hesitation. It paralyzed him until I went over and helped him down from the roof. And that was the last time we ever played this game together.

It was inevitable that this moment would one day arrive but I wonder if God too has such memories of times when we have chosen fear over faith. Does the Lord remember the first time He saw us hedging our bets, or setting up a back-up plan just in case He didn't come through for us? Might this apply to something that God is presently inviting you to trust Him with? If so what would it take for you to return to that child-like trust where, without hesitation, you would gladly jump into God's arms?

To exercise trust in God is to express faith that God's character is good, that He is up for the task, and that we expect Him to be faithful to His word. It also honours God that we are at peace in the certainty that He has our best interests in mind. Trusting God then is the most direct means we have of honouring His character. And the many ways by which we express such confidence in God's faithfulness are surely what most touches our Father's heart.

17

We have much to say about this, but it is hard to make it clear to you because you no longer try to understand.

Heb. 5:11

We know very little about the recipients of the letter to the Hebrews other than that, having taken the first steps towards maturity in Christ, they've now taken a step back. According to Heb. 5:11, they "no longer try to understand." Another way to translate the Greek phrase used here is that they have become "dull with respect to what is heard." In other words they hear without effect, without enthusiasm or response. Immune to the word of God, they no longer feel the same need for conversion as they once did. No longer do they expect any real challenge or motivation from the Holy Spirit's prompting, and the writer rebukes them for this when he says, "though by this time you ought to be teachers, you need someone to teach you the elementary truths of God's word all over again" (Heb. 5:12). He compares their immaturity to a baby who drinks only milk.

Milk is best for a baby because it can't handle solid foods. But to continue with milk once it is old enough for a solid diet would not be good. Not only would it stunt its growth but the baby would always be hungry and unsatisfied as its body craved something more substantial. So it is with the recipients of this letter. They have not progressed to the solid food they should be enjoying by now, and they risk spiritual anemia because of their impoverished diet.

Unfortunately this is also what we see in too many Christians today. There is a malaise or discouragement among many who grieve that they no longer feel what they used to feel when they were young in the faith. They no longer enjoy the same enthusiasm for worship, preaching, prayer or Scripture as they once did. And though they grieve their loss of passion, they are no longer sure what to hope for other than an impossible return to where they once were. They are hungry for something more and often feel guilty, believing that this hunger is a sign of their failure to secure the promises they once believed were possible. And so they find themselves either living in a constant state of dissatisfaction, or else lowering their expectations of the spiritual life to something more in line with their experience. Either way they remain unsatisfied because they know they are no longer thriving as they once were.

The writer of Hebrews warns us of such pitfalls if we do not "hold firmly to the end the confidence we had at first" (Heb. 3:14). If we do not continually expect more of the spiritual life, we too will risk similar disappointment. We are exhorted instead to show diligence in seeking God so that none of us miss out on the promises that still lay ahead of us. There is more gold in the ground, and we are encouraged to keep digging until we find it.

18

"My Father, if it is not possible for this cup to be taken away
unless I drink it, may your will be done."

Mat. 26:42

In the story of Gethsemane recorded in Matthew's gospel, Jesus acknowledges His wish that the occasion for His suffering would be removed. Like any of us confronted by unwanted circumstances the Lord prays, as we have perhaps often prayed ourselves, "My Father, if it is possible, may this cup be taken from me. "

Jesus tables His preference. But He does so in the posture of a servant who defers to the will of his master as He adds the courageous footnote, "Yet not as I will, but as you will." As disagreeable as it is to His human nature, if He must drink the bitter cup, Jesus is prepared to accept His Father's will.

How often, in our own lives, have we too prayed in the hope that "this cup be taken from me?" But what happens when God does not answer this prayer? Where do we go when it becomes apparent that the cup of suffering will not pass? Jesus faced this reality in Gethsemane and altered His prayer accordingly. In a rephrasing of His first petition He models for us a disposition that we too might claim when the cup we wish were taken away from us does not pass.

In Matthew's account of Gethsemane, Jesus prays three times. The wording of his first petition, "if it is possible, may this cup be taken from me," changes in His second and third prayers to the more resigned, "if it is not possible for this cup to be taken away unless I drink it, may your will be done." Jesus' prayer evolves from one that expresses His natural and understandable aversion to suffering, to one that now prepares Him for the fate He must accept. It is a prayer that seeks the grace to endure what cannot be changed.

Such prayers apply to us as well in every anticipated suffering. We pray, naturally, for the removal of such if possible, but we must also pray beyond this first objective. If the only petition we make is that suffering be taken from us we will find ourselves dismayed should the cup remain. Our petition will seem to have failed and God will seem to have deserted us. We must also be prepared to courageously pray, as Jesus did, "if this cup cannot pass unless I drink it, let your will be done."

The Lord did not hide from us His aversion to suffering. The cup, as we know, was not taken from Him. But what did pass was the fear that it produced in Him. Whether the cup of suffering is taken away from us or must remain until we drink it, our best hope lies in the same assurance that Jesus draws courage from—that, either way, this cup will surely pass.

19

God has given us his very great and precious promises, so that through them we may participate in the divine nature.

2 Pet 1:4

Makarios the Great was a Syrian spiritual director who ministered in the fourth century near the border area of Cappadocia (Turkey) and

Syria. He was a disciple of St. Antony, the first of the desert fathers. In his teachings, Makarios often stressed the importance of a felt experience of God. He saw this as an indicator of the Holy Spirit, through whom we come to "taste and see that the Lord is good" (Ps. 34:8). Such foretastes of God cause us to grow in our desire to be united with God as the object of our love.

For most early theologians, the highest expression and purpose of faith was the union of the soul with God. This is why God became man through Jesus—to unite Himself to our humanity so that our humanity could be united with His divinity. As Makarios taught, "The infinite God diminished Himself in order to be united with His creatures, so they can be made participators of divine life."

The apostle Peter, as well, teaches that God's promises in Christ—in whom the fullness of both humanity and divinity are joined—represent an invitation to "participate in the divine nature" (2Pet 1:4). And we do so by simply submitting our lives to the Holy Spirit, which is why theologians often refer to the third person of the Trinity as "the agent of our participation." Spiritual maturity then is the fruit of our ongoing response to the Spirit's invitation which we participate in through the yielding of our hearts.

One of Makarios' most memorable metaphors for the passive way we make ourselves available to the Holy Spirit is that of the heart serving as a "resonating chamber." In the same way that the body of a guitar or a violin serves to amplify the sound of the plucked or bowed string, so our bodies become a place where the song of the Spirit re-sonates within us. He writes,

> As breath sounds when passed through a flute, so does the Holy
> Spirit make music in the holy and God-bearing saints who, from
> a pure heart, become hymns and psalms to God.

Echoing the insight of other desert saints, Makarios recognizes the resulting "music" as that of the Holy Spirit lifting us up in the praise of God. It is the Spirit within us—the "Word" which does not come back empty— who returns praise to Christ through the instrument of our yielded hearts. As Makarios expresses,

> The Spirit, taking possession of the soul, now sings a new song to
> the Lord with the timbrel of the body and so it sends up praises,
> through the believer, to the life-giving Christ.

If such be the case, all the more should our desire be to make room for the Holy Spirit's resonance in our souls. Let us heed the Psalmist's call to worship when he says: "Awake my soul! Sing and make music to your God. Let us offer our hearts as instruments of His praise."

20

To the one who does not work but trusts God who justifies
the ungodly, their faith is credited as righteousness.

Rom. 4:5

In her biography, *Before the Living God*, the Carmelite Abbess Ruth Burrows writes about the pilgrimage of trust that she and her fellow sisters have long been on. She sees the development of our growing trust in God as the principle agenda of the spiritual life, something that we can only enjoy to the degree that we have put to rest the anxious "work" of trying to manage our relationship with God. She writes,

> I want to show people that what really matters is utter trust in God; that this trust cannot be there until we have lost all self-trust and are rooted in poverty; that we must be willing to go to God with empty hands. The whole meaning of our existence and the one consuming desire of the heart of God is that we should trust God enough to let ourselves be loved.

Trusting God's love for us means doing so in the context of our sense of personal inadequacy, especially with regards to the spiritual life. To fret over our failures, or to presume that these disqualify us in any way, is to usurp God's prerogative to love us even in our poverty.

As a young nun observing her fellow sisters, Burrows remembers the many so-called spiritual acts that, in her estimation, revealed more of a lack of trust among those who had otherwise committed their lives so wholly to God. She writes,

> Looking at my dear friends, living for God, I saw in fact that something was yet wanting in them. They had not yet come to perfect trust. They felt they were spiritual failures because this or that had not happened to them. They felt they had missed out on something because their experience carried none of the features they assumed a truly authentic spiritual life should yield.

It is this nagging sense that we are never spiritual enough that reveals our lack of trust in God. As we chase the spiritual life like a carrot at the end of a stick we never get to truly rest in God's present love for us. Concerning her friends Burrows adds,

> They knew they were loved by God and yet there was an indefinable anxiety which inhibited their total surrender to that love. I saw these dear people, self-giving, generous, full of love for God and yet still anxious, still hesitant before the last step which would release them from themselves and open them to God's love.

Far from criticizing the weakness of human faith, Burrows writes with compassion as a co-captive who is just beginning to feel the bindings of her own fears giving way. She longs to instill this hope in others as well. She writes,

> I long to convince them that, here and now, in their present 'unsatisfactory' state, in their so-called 'failure', God desires to give himself to them; that this state of poverty is precisely what he wants and that it represents his way into them. He has laboured with love for a long time to open up this way for them. Will they now block it? If they do, they are turning from the straight path of poverty, and choosing instead the winding road of spiritual riches.

Burrows clearly understands the sufficiency of Jesus' word, "Blessed are the poor in spirit" (Mt. 5:3). She is convinced, as we should be, that if God truly blesses our poverty, His promises are in no way hindered by our failure to deserve them.

> *Let the one who walks in the dark, who has no light, trust in the name of the LORD and rely on their God.*

Isa. 50:10

21

"If you call the Sabbath a delight
and the LORD's holy day honorable...,
then you will find your joy in the LORD.

Isa. 58:13-14

The Bible, on the whole, is more concerned with time than with space. It pays more attention to events, and is more concerned with history than with geography or sacred places. That's what made Judaism so different from other ancient near-east religions. It is a religion of time that aims at the sanctification of time.

The idea that holiness might be found in geography, or in nature, was a common concept in ancient near-east religions. Mountains, streams, trees, caves, certain animals and plants were all considered, by some, to be holy. New in the teaching of Israel was the idea that time could be seen as holy. It was a shift from the realm of nature to the realm of history, from things to events. For the Israelite there were no sacred plants, animals, or caves. Instead they were introduced to sacred events which they were to commemorate, like the Exodus, and to a sacred day they were to honour called the Sabbath. For Israel it was not the physical world that was the shrine of the divine, it was time.

The Jewish theologian Abraham Heschel reminds us that the first thing to be called holy in all of creation, was not a people, or a place, but a day—the Sabbath. The Episcopal priest, Barbara Brown Taylor writes similarly,

> God worked hard for six days and then God rested, performing the consummate act of divine freedom by doing nothing at all. Furthermore, the rest was so delicious that God did not call it good, or even very good. Instead, God blessed the seventh day and called it holy, making Sabbath the first sacred thing in all creation.

According to Heschel, this is what makes the Sabbath a "palace in time"—a non-physical cathedral into which human beings are invited to return every week of their lives. It represents not so much a place but an opening of time in which we are to seek and encounter God. On the Sabbath, we live our day under the canopy of holy time.

Sabbath therefore is not something we do, but more a God-given time that we are invited to enter—to discover ourselves *within* the Sabbath. To honour the Sabbath then is to live receptively within a set-aside time that God recognizes and blesses as holy. A day to receive the particular blessing that God has prepared for us from the beginning of time.

> *To God who rested from all action on the seventh day*
> *and ascended upon His throne of glory,*
> *He vested the day of rest with beauty;*
> *He called the Sabbath a delight.*
> *...The seventh day itself is uttering praise.*
> *the Sabbath day sings:*
> *"It is good to give thanks unto the Lord!"*

-Sabbath Morning Prayer

22

When someone invites you to a wedding feast, do not take the place of honor, for a person more distinguished than you may have been invited. If so, the host who invited both of you will come and say to you, 'Give this person your seat.' Then, humiliated, you will have to take the least important place. But when you are invited, take the lowest place, so that when your host comes, he will say to you, 'Friend, move up to a better place.' Then you will be honored in the presence of all the other guests. For all those who exalt themselves will be humbled, and those who humble themselves will be exalted.

Luke 14:7-11

Many Christians suffer much more than they need to with the guilt of failure, especially as it applies to their spiritual lives. They presume that everyone else is doing well in their faith, but that somehow it hasn't taken root in them as it should have. And they blame themselves in the belief that they have not tried hard enough, or have not been faithful enough to the call, or strong enough in their desires for God. In short, they feel they have failed to become the Christians they had once thought, or been told, was possible for them. If this, in any way, describes your experience of faith, Jesus has a parable for you that comes with an unexpected word of counsel for high-achiever Christians: "You need to lower the bar of your self-expectations."

Though it might sound negligent, we are always wrong to set the bar of our spiritual expectations too high. To believe that virtue, steadfastness, sanctity and godly love are all within our reach is a temptation of pride. And, if we are honest with ourselves, the disappointment that inevitably results has little to do with God. It is mostly related to our disappointment with ourselves. We have spurned the blessed humility of our poverty of spirit, and have rather believed the devil's lie that "ye shall be as gods." In other words, we have been presumptuous about our potential status in the kingdom, assuming that a place of honour should be more natural to us than a lower seat.

As Jesus makes clear in this parable, we are best to set the bar of our self-expectations quite low. We are, after all, not "as gods." Rather, we are very much the blind, the lost, the faithless and the hearts of stone that Christ has come to save. And we do well to not forget the humility of who we truly are.

Perhaps the best indicator of whether our bar is set too high lies in how we respond to our seeming successes or failures. Which do we seem most surprised about— that we have failed to be genuine in our spirituality, or that we have succeeded? With the bar of our expectations inordinately high, we will often be dismayed that we have not achieved what we thought we were capable of. Our pride will see this as failure and we will respond with shame. But if we accept the humbling truth that the bar of our capacity is actually quite low we will be much more disposed to surprise. We will more readily marvel at the grace of God that allows us, at times, to be much more righteous than we know ourselves to be. No longer will we see virtue as a personal achievement, but more as the gift of God's grace that it truly is.

Jesus concludes His teaching with a simple formula: "all those who exalt themselves will be humbled, and those who humble themselves will be exalted." This is certainly good news for anyone who is ready to embrace the blessed humility of their creatureliness as both the starting and end point of their spiritual life.

23

Break up your fallow ground, for it is time to seek the LORD until He comes to rain righteousness on you.

Hos. 10:12 (NRSV)

Each winter as the ice thickened on the St. Lawrence River, I remember watching the small fishing huts being set up for the season. Some were simple shacks, no larger than an outhouse. Others were quite elaborate in construction, with shelves, coat hooks, heaters and even bedding. The central feature in each of these huts though, from the most modest to the most extravagant, was the hole in the ice. This hole represented the very purpose of the shack being there. It was a fishing hole, cut with an auger and then enlarged with a saw until it was big enough not only for your fishing line, but hopefully to pull a large fish through its opening and into your net.

Once dug, the hole served its purpose for the day. But as fishermen returned in the morning, the first order of the day was always the same—to cut through the ice that had re-formed over the hole during the night. Luckily it was thin ice and could be easily broken with a stick. But if it had been a few days since the hut was used, the ice would naturally be thicker. A small stick would no longer do the job. And if the fisherman had not remembered to bring an axe with him, he would not be able to fish that day.

Something similar takes place in us with regards to the "hole" that prayer creates in us each day. By God's grace, we return to a place of sensitive relationship with the humble truth of who we are. As prayer creates such openness in us, our hearts seem to flow more freely. But, between prayer times, we can often sense the ice re-forming over this hole, blocking, in our experience at least, our sense of access to God or to the truth of our more profound selves. And if we have been absent from prayer for a length of time it can well seem that only an axe could cut through the thickness of the impasse we feel.

Our sensitivity to the Holy Spirit is not something we can presume upon. We are wise therefore to return to prayer each day in order to keep our lines of communication with God open and unobstructed—to make sure that the "ice" does not thicken around our heart and block its flow. "Break up your fallow ground" Hosea tells us. But maturity teaches us to also respect the ounce of prevention that will keep the ground from overly hardening in the first place.

24

God disciplines us for our good, in order that we may share in his holiness. No discipline seems pleasant at the time, but painful. Later on, however, it produces a harvest of righteousness and peace for those who have been trained by it.

Heb. 12:10-11

When it comes to our relationship to the gospel, we often find ourselves in an impoverished state, never able to accumulate enough insight, or enough experience to make us feel that we ever have the upper hand in any of this. As P. T. Forsyth writes in his classic book, *The Soul of Prayer*, "the more we grasp the gospel, the more it abases us."

We are constantly being undone by the gospel. It is always pruning us in order that we might live more faithfully in the humility of its truth. Forsyth expands on this saying,

> The gospel is continually acting on us, continually searching our inner selves, so that no part of us may be unforgiven, unfed, or unsanctified. We cannot hold it and examine it at arm's length. It enters into us. It evokes a perpetual comment on our souls, and puts us continually on self-judgment.

Odd as it might seem, the increasing scrutiny and conviction of the Holy Spirit is actually good news. What it cultivates in us is not so much an expertise in the ways of virtue, but more the resignation of faith that trusts, in spite of all evidence, that God's sanctifying work is actually taking place in us. Forsyth offers us hope in this when he writes,

> There is no real intimacy with the gospel which does not mean a new sense of God's holiness, and it may be long before we realize that the same holiness that abases is that which saves us.

We are invited to embrace this humbling action of God's Spirit in the knowledge that everything that rebukes our self-satisfaction does still more to draw out our faith. Our continual sense of falling short can often seem like a sign of failure, but the opposite is actually true—the more God humbles us, the more deeply we carry the evidence of His sanctifying work in our lives.

Maturity, then, will not only anticipate this abasing action of the gospel but will actually welcome it. It will embrace its sacred effects and desire the humility that it purposes in us. Knowing that it is for the healing of our souls that the Holy Spirit enables us, we will position ourselves all the more to receive this ministry. As P.T. Forsyth concludes, "We are not the fire, but we should do all we can to live where it burns."

> *Amid the wreck of my little world He is firm, and I in Him. I justify God even in the ruins; in His good time I shall arrive.*
>
> P. T. Forsyth

25

Martha was distracted by all the preparations that had to be made. She came to Jesus and asked, "Lord, don't you care that my sister has left me to do the work by myself? Tell her to help me!"

Luke 10:40

Teresa of Avila offers a wonderful teaching on spiritual maturity that relates to the story of Mary and Martha. In it she recognizes the tension between these two sisters as representative of the same tensions we often feel between our active and passive dispositions. She also speaks of the maturity that will inevitably bring both these spiritual dispositions together to form a graced whole in our lives.

Martha had a good work ethic. Unfortunately, it was also the reason for her missing out on a deeper relationship with Jesus. Though she likely accomplished much in her day, it was at the expense of something even more important in her life. Ironically, it was because Martha was busy doing things *for* Jesus that she ended up missing out on Jesus Himself.

We can easily recognize this same tendency in ourselves, which is why we feel such empathy for Martha when Jesus affirms her sister's disposition over hers. The likelihood that Martha would have preferred to be with Jesus is implied in the resentment she expresses. Mary, after all, is sitting there enjoying what Martha would also like to enjoy, but doing so at the expense of her household responsibilities. And yet Jesus tells Martha that her sister has chosen the better thing.

We can assume that Jesus is not telling Martha that there is anything wrong with the work she is doing. Nor is He suggesting that Mary should be exempt from such work, or that we too should drop out of the active life in order to sit at His feet all day. There is something else going on here that has more to do with the ordering of our affections than with the work we do.

Teresa of Avila recognizes how both the active and passive sides of our spiritual life must eventually come together. The initial spiritual direction, for most of us, is to grow from the disposition of Martha, whose active life distracts her from the presence of God, to the "better choice" that Mary represents, where another priority has been assumed. More important than anything we do for Christ is the better choice of simply being with Christ.

But, for Teresa, this corrective is not an end in itself. She understands that the active life will always be the norm. But, for the mature Christian, it will be so in a new way. We will no longer be active at the expense of our contemplative nature. Our work will no longer take us away from Christ but will now just be another arena through which we contemplate the living and active presence of God in our day.

Spiritual maturity will ultimately represent a combination of both Mary and Martha's dispositions. In Teresa's memorable words, "The mature soul will live both the active and the contemplative life at the same time. It will be active in the world and yet understand that the best part of the soul is somewhere else."

> By the grace of God I am what I am, and his grace to me was not without effect. No, I worked harder than all of them—yet not I, but the grace of God that was with me.
>
> 1Cor. 15:10

26

*You study the Scriptures diligently because you think that
in them you have eternal life. These are the very
Scriptures that testify about me, yet you refuse to come to
me to have life.*

John 5:39-40

Speaking to those who had spent many hours studying the Hebrew Scriptures, Jesus suggests a more direct route. It seems that, for these scribes, their study of God was actually eclipsing the more immediate relationship that Jesus was encouraging them to receive. How does this word apply to us as well? How, for instance, might the many spiritual books we read become a substitute for living more directly with God? Jesus seems to imply that this can easily happen.

Books certainly stimulate our prayer but they can also become a substitute for it. They can fill up spaces of longing within us that God would rather keep empty. They can also prevent us from entering the more arid places of purification that God would lead us to as He encourages us to face our true poverty of spirit.

Anthony Bloom, a contemporary Orthodox bishop, is certainly among those who would encourage a more frugal approach to God. He stresses the importance of knowing who we are apart from any outside stimulus. Bloom even recommends boredom as a God-given means by which we come to terms with the radical nakedness of our being. He writes,

> Try to find time to stay alone with yourself, doing nothing. Discover boredom; discover how little we have to offer to ourselves as food for thought, for emotion and for life.

Our culture is so heavily invested in outside stimulation that we rarely have to face the full poverty of our inner life. But outside stimulus, even if it is religious or devotional, cannot fully satisfy our deep longings for God. In placating our hunger for God, such indirect encounter can actually dissipate the more intense longing that is meant to grow in us. As Bloom writes, "Very often we do not find sufficient intensity in our prayer, sufficient conviction, or sufficient faith, because our despair is not deep enough."

True prayer comes from true need. That is why under-stimulation—

silence, solitude, fasting, poverty, etc.—has always been the prescribed way for saints to grow in the recognition of their deep and existential need for God. But places of under-stimulation also represent deserts that most of us will do anything to avoid. Bloom offers what might seem like an extreme recommendation to counter our addictions to stimulus when he writes,

> Be patient about prayer. Wait until the longing for God is sincere, until you get that desperate feeling in your heart that says, 'I am alone, where is He?' Stay the course until the anguish so fills our mind, our heart, and our will with a sense that unless God comes I am lost, there is no hope. To return to activity without God will be to return to the realm of delusion, of reflected life, but not to real life.

We must have faith that a blessing actually awaits us on the other side of extended silence and solitude before we will ever subject ourselves to such deprivation. But it is only in facing our true selves in the absence of external stimulus that we will ever realize how little there is within us to satisfy our spirituality. At this point, we just might come to God with a more genuine appreciation of how much our lives truly depend on His.

> *The bold demand of the soul that climbs the hills of desire*
> *tends towards the direct knowledge and enjoyment of God,*
> *and not merely one that comes through mirrors or*
> *reflections.*
>
> St. Gregory of Nyssa

27

Take my yoke upon you…and you will find rest for your souls.

Matt. 11:29

The burdens of life are heavier whenever we feel more alone with them than we need to. We take on too much when we face ourselves or our circumstances on our own. We are meant, rather, to be yoked with Jesus as our first relationship, and then to all else secondly.

Whether it is to an action that needs to be done, or to a person or problem we are relating to, we always assume more responsibility than necessary when we approach these things alone. Most Christians will naturally include God at some point in these relationships, but often only by implication. The focus too often remains primarily between ourselves and the thing we are relating to, with God more often on the periphery.

The diagram below depicts something of this relationship, where God is more in the background than should be (the dotted line being the implied relationship, and the solid line the direct one).

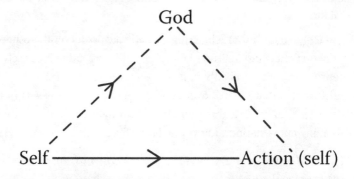

Scripture however would have us first be yoked with Jesus and then, together with Jesus, form a relationship to our action or to ourselves. No longer facing life alone, we then approach all things together with Christ. The following diagram illustrates this difference, where our primary relationship is to God and then, together with God, we address whatever else we face in life.

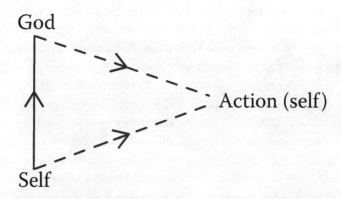

To always be mindful of God as our first axis of relationship is a difficult posture to maintain. When the stakes or the demands of life seem high we often fixate more directly on the things we are related to. We leave our primary bearings with God, and end up more yoked with our selves than with Christ.

It takes discipline to establish this truth as a constant in our lives. But there is no other way. We must choose between Jesus' yoke or our curious preference for facing life alone. And, as Scripture promises, only the former can free us from the unnecessary burdens we will otherwise assume are ours alone to bear.

28

When he finally came to his senses....

Luke 15:7

How long do you think it must've taken for the story of the prodigal son to unfold? From the time he left his father's house, to that fateful day when he ended up in a pig sty, how much time has likely passed? 3 years? 5 years? 10 years? How fast can you spend that much money? For the sake of argument, let's say this all took place over a five year period. What might some of the likely stages of decline and denial have been before the son finally came to his senses and realized the truth of his predicament? Let's start with the first year.

Imagine how it must have felt for the son in the initial year, having asked for, and received not only his freedom from family responsibilities, but also a large sum of cash to go with it. He had asked for an advance on his inheritance, and, to his great surprise, his father had actually agreed. He got what he wanted, with very little effort on his part. Echoing words that the Israelites had once said to God—"we are free to roam, we will come to you no more" (Jer. 2:31)—he packed his bags and left home.

I can imagine the son being quite pleased with himself as he looked back at his father's estate. He had everything he needed to make his mark in the world. And for the next year or so, he probably had a pretty good time of it. Oblivious to the reality of his dwindling resources he spent his money without thought of consequence.

A year passed. And then another one. By year three, did he even notice that his debts had grown to surpass the money he had left? After years of burying his head in the sand, there must've come a day when it finally dawned on him that there was a real problem here. But was this the end of the story? Not likely. Like an alcoholic who hasn't hit bottom, how much longer did it take before the prodigal son got to the final stage of accepting ownership of his problem? And how much later was it before he actually did something about it? Another year? Maybe more? In spite of increasing evidence of a crisis looming, he likely continued to deny his predicament—until it was too late. His back against the wall, he was left with only a few dismal choices.

Why did it take so long, and the final degradation of a pig sty, before the prodigal son finally came to his senses? Why was he unable to recognize that his branch was withering? What contributed to this wilful blindness? These are questions we need to ask ourselves as well. We as well know of correctives that God is calling us to make in our lives. In what ways are we, like the prodigal son, denying or putting them off? In what ways do we keep rationalizing that we have more time to deal with a bad situation than we really do? In other words, what prevents us from "coming to our senses" earlier?

If we are open to such questions we will have opportunity to avert the unnecessary suffering that our refusal to accept the uncomfortable truths of life will otherwise bring. With an ounce of prevention we might save ourselves the pound of cure that the pig sty will otherwise represent for us. And if we can start working on solutions long before we've run out of credible options we can hopefully avoid the predicament of having life force changes on us that we knew we should've made ourselves years ago.

29

He says, "Be still, and know that I am God;
I will be exalted among the nations,
I will be exalted in the earth."

Psalm 46:10

"Be still and know that I am God." It is a beautiful verse that we often repeat to ourselves? We sing it in hymns, recite it in liturgies, engrave it on coffee cups and embroider it on doilies. It is a word that brings comfort as a gentle invitation from the Lord to come away and get to know Him better.

But the actual context of this phrase in Psalm 46 is quite different from the sentiment we usually associate with it. The verse is actually a rebuke to warring nations, and to every turmoil and fear of life that raises itself above the legitimate supremacy of God. In no uncertain terms the Lord makes clear that this must stop. In the face of all such presumption He asserts Himself declaring, "I *will* be exalted."

Psalm 46 addresses the nations that are in uproar. But this word also speaks to any form of turmoil that exalts itself, in our minds at least, above God. It applies to our inner life, to our marriages, our businesses and our church communities— any place where the fears of life or the imperatives of the self are exalted above the sovereignty of God.

The Lord issues this word as a strong command, "Be still." It is not meant to be a gentle word. Rather it is God rebuking the fears and useless anxieties that hold His people captive. To all such spirits the Lord says, "It is *I* who will be exalted in this person's life, not you." It is a word that applies to any area of our lives where we have evidently forgotten God and now find ourselves bound to the self-acting soul.

"Be still and know that I am God." This is a saving word. It is the Lord reasserting His claim on our lives, rebuking all the turmoil in and around us and saying, "You have exalted your fearful imaginings above my sovereignty. Now be still and remember I am God." Jesus spoke these very same words to the stormy seas, and just as it did for the waves, it is a command that brings peace and the restoration of right relationship to our souls and, ultimately, to the whole world.

> *Jesus got up, rebuked the wind and said to the waves, "Quiet! Be still!" Then the wind died down and it was completely calm.*
>
> Mark 4:39

30

> *The Lord said to me, "You are my servant,*
> *Israel, in whom I will display my splendour."*
> *But I said, "I have laboured in vain;*
> *I have spent my strength for nothing at all.*
> *Yet what is due me is in the LORD's hand,*
> *and my reward is with my God."*
>
> Isaiah 49:3-4

These verses read like a three-act play. They represent a dialogue similar to many of our ongoing discussions with God. The progression of this play could be summarized as follows:

- Act 1) The way God sees us.
- Act 2) The way we see ourselves.
- Act 3) Accepting God's vision of us as more true than our own.

In the first act, the Lord declares to His servants that His splendour is displayed in their lives. Similar things are said of us throughout Scripture. Jesus tells us for instance that, "You are the light of the world." Peter affirms us as "a royal priesthood." Paul tells us that we are a temple in which God's Spirit dwells. The problem is that it sounds too good to be true, which leads us to the next verse.

In the second act we find ourselves disputing such claims. We respond according to our own self-assessment, saying to God, "I have achieved nothing and all I have laboured for has been in vain." Leaning on our own understanding we see ourselves as falling far short of anything we think God envisions for us. And to the degree that we rely on our own perception, rather than on God's, we feel discouraged about our spiritual lives. No longer do we recognize the splendour that God sees. Our focus instead is fixed on the many ways we are apparently missing the mark of our calling.

But the third act resolves the play by re-establishing the truth of our lives according to God's first vision. We are re-instated as the sons and daughters of the Most High, not because we have tried harder to be who we think we should be, or that we have somehow achieved the high hopes we had for our spirituality. Our re-instatement is now the result of our simply deferring to God's vision—believing His word more than our own. We have come to accept, as the Psalmist does, that "what is due me is in the Lord's hand." In other words, "I am whatever God judges me to be."

In John 15:3 Jesus tells us, "You are clean because of the word I spoke to you." Who are we to argue with this Divine verdict? God likewise tells me that His splendour is being displayed in my life. He seems delighted by this fact. Whether I can see or accept the truth of this is largely inconsequential to the validity of the Lord's declaration. For "as He judges me, so I am."

And as the Psalmist recognizes, whatever my labour has been, the fruit of my reward lies solely with God. May we too find our truest sense of self through the Lord's eyes, more than through our own.

31

Find rest, O my soul, in God alone;
   my hope comes from him.
He alone is my rock and my salvation;
   he is my fortress, I will not be shaken.

Psalm 62:5-8

There is a progression that takes place in the unfolding narrative of most of our conversion stories. Generally speaking we go from having virtually no relationship with God, to a partial relationship, and then finally to a fully committed relationship. And according to this psalm, a fully committed relationship to God is not measured by how much we do for God, but by how fully we depend on Him for the security and definition of our lives.

The Psalmist epitomizes the final stage of this conversion with the concise phrase, "He *alone* is my rock." It describes a mature spirituality that not only recognizes the sufficiency of God, but actually celebrates the posture of dependence that this sufficiency implies. The mark of a growing spirituality then is that the more mature we are in our faith, the greater dependence on God we should be experiencing.

Our conversion from "no dependence" to "full dependence" on God represents a gradual exchange of our securities. We surrender the confidence we have in our own ways in favour of a more trusting relationship with the mysterious and unknown ways of God. Though it seems at first like a precarious choice, this conversion will lead us from the false self to the true self, from a life burdened by its own devices to a life more fully yoked with Christ's.

Most of us must confess however that, at best, we are only partially given to God. He is not the only rock that we lean on. Rather than rest in the dependent posture that our creature-Creator relationship demands we stubbornly cling to our false sense of in-dependence. This is our confession—that we are only partially given to God. And the sooner we accept this truth, the more focussed our spiritual direction will be.

The person who is truly dependent on the Lord is one who is firmly rooted in faith. Their lives are now established (i.e. made stable) in Christ (Rom. 16:25, Eph. 3:17). No longer shaken by circumstances, or tossed to and fro by the pros and cons of their own perceptions, they rest more solidly on the Rock of their salvation.

"Find rest, o my soul, in God alone." This is the wisdom the Psalmist prescribes for us. We are to assure our souls—in spite of our self-doubt and the need for self-protection we otherwise feel necessary—that this option is our wisest choice. And to the degree that our souls respond to this invitation we will enjoy the reward of its promise—we will stand among the very few men and women on earth who can say with confidence, "The Lord is my Rock. I will not be shaken."

32

Who is it he is trying to teach? To whom is he explaining his message? To children weaned from their milk, to those just taken from the breast? For it is: "Do and do, do and do, rule on rule, rule on rule; a little here, a little there."
Very well then, with foreign lips and strange tongues
God will speak to this people, to whom he said,
"This is the resting place, let the weary rest";
and, "This is the place of repose"— but they would
not listen.

Isaiah 28:9-12

There is a repeated theme throughout Scripture that has to do with the invitation (or more often the command) for us to rest in God. Jesus, for instance, instructs us to take on His yoke so that we will find rest for our souls (Mat. 11:28). His invitation, is given to us in positive terms. But more often we see a similar exhortation in Scripture followed by either a warning or else an expression of God's disappointment in our refusal to obey this ordinance to rest in Him.

The book of Hebrews, for instance, describes a "Sabbath rest that awaits the children of God" (Heb. 4:9). It encourages us to "make every effort to enter this rest (Heb. 4:11). But it also warns against our refusing this invitation, charging those who do so with disobedience, akin to the Israelites' rebellion at Meribah. (Heb. 3:15, Ps. 95:7-11)

We are familiar as well with Isaiah's verse where God tells us that "in repentance and rest is your salvation, in quietness and trust is your strength" (Isa. 30:15) But do we also remember the convicting phrase that follows this verse: "But you would have none of it?" The Lord is dismayed by our refusal to accept such a gracious offering.

Elsewhere, in Jeremiah, we are told to "ask where the good way is, and walk in it," counsel that comes with a promise that we will then "find rest for our souls" (Jer. 6:16). But once again, we hear the Lord's disappointment with our refusal to accept this invitation, "But you said, "We will not walk in it."

And finally, in our passage from Isaiah 28, God invites us to Himself saying, "This is the resting place, let the weary rest. This is the place of repose." And once again we hear God's discouragement at our response when He adds, "but they would not listen."

To refuse God's rest is seen in Scripture as not only a loss for us, but also as an act of childish rebellion. It grieves the Lord who is disappointed by the immaturity that this represents. God expects us to heed His call but, in respect of the freedom He has given us, He also allows us to disobey. He lets us go our own way. In the language of Rom. 1:24, the Lord "gives us over" to the frenetic life that our rebellious choices inspire. Isaiah describes this self-prescribed life as one defined by imperatives this way, "therefore, the word of the Lord will become for them: "Do and do, do and do, rule on rule, rule on rule." It is an indictment that describes too well the oppressive lives many Christians are living today.

The Lord "agrees to disagree" with us by letting us taste the consequences of our disobedience. But though He "gives us over" to our own way, God surely wishes it were otherwise—that we would simply heed His counsel and enter His rest.

33

I am going away and I am coming back to you.

John 14:28

It is a common feature of the spiritual life to experience what seem like the comings and goings of God. Evidently it is God's prerogative to either reveal or conceal Himself as He chooses. Such was the experience of the prophet Isaiah when he observed that, "Surely you are a God who hides Himself" (Isa. 45:15). It was also the experience of Bernard de Clairvaux, the 12th century abbot and spiritual director who wrote,

> The Word, which is Christ, comes and goes as He pleases. At least that is how the soul perceives it. The soul notices the Word is with her. When she is not aware of His presence, she thinks of Him as absent and begs for his return. She is not calling out for a first experience but cries instead, "Turn! Come back!"

Perhaps one of the reasons God appears to leave us is to simply make His presence all the more desirable. Bernard offers two examples in Scripture that seem to suggest this. There is the story of Jesus walking on the water who, after the disciples recognize Him, acts as though He is going to pass them by (Mark 6:48-49). Then there is the story of the Lord arriving at Emmaus with the other two disciples. He then continues walking "as if He were going farther" (Luke 24:29). Bernard writes,

> The impression that He was about to pass by them was only a holy feigning. He did it to help them. The Lord behaves in the same way with the soul that loves Him. He seems willing to pass by, only to excite a prayer for Him to return.

There is great mystery in how the Lord elicits our loving response through His seeming absence. No one can anticipate His arrival, nor can our grasping prevent His leaving. Such was Bernard's experience of the Holy Spirit's coming and going in his own life. He writes,

> He has come to me on numerous occasions. I never notice the precise moment when He arrives. I feel His presence and then I remember that He was with me. Sometimes I have a premonition that He is coming to me. But I have never been able to put my finger on the exact instant when He arrived or departed. As the Psalmist says, "His footsteps are not known" (Ps. 77:19).

How then are we to recognize God's presence in our prayers? We will know, evidently, by the fruit it bears in us. The effects of the Spirit are the obvious signs of His having "visited" us. Bernard writes,

> How then did I know He was in me? I couldn't miss it! It affected me in an undeniable way. My heart was softened and my soul roused from its slumber. He went to work in me. He cleared and cultivated the soil of my soul. He planted and watered and brought light to dark places. He opened what was closed and warmed what was cold.

God's presence with us is recognized by the effects it has on our will, as well as the healing it produces in our souls. As Bernard notes,

> It was the warmth of my heart that made me know he had completely flooded my being. Personal flaws became unimportant. Every desire was controlled. My slightest intention to do better was met with kindness and mercy. I have seen a fraction of his glory and it is awesome.

The opposite, of course, is also true. When we sense that God has "left us," we naturally grieve having to return to our more diminished self.

Bernard describes his own sense of spiritual loss saying,

> When the Word departs, these things cool. It's like taking a boiling pot away from the fire. There can be no doubt that the experience is gone. Sorrow is automatic. But when it returns, I feel the warmth, and I know once again that He is with me.

There is a proper season for every experience of God. The spiritually mature Christian must learn to accept the subtle and creative artistry of God's ways. For reasons known only to Himself, the Lord graces us at times with seasons of spiritual abundance, and at other times with seasons of spiritual aridity. And both these experiences can serve to purify the sincerity of our love.

34

Come now, and let us reason together.

Isaiah 1:18

My high school English teacher taught us a very important lesson in how to cultivate a fruitful relationship with any subject matter He taught us how to ask intelligent questions. Every Friday, instead of giving the class a test, he would simply hand out blank sheets of paper and have us write three thoughtful questions concerning whatever book we were studying. His premise was that, unless you have given serious thought to a subject matter, you can't ask intelligent questions about it.

In his book, *Spiritual Direction*, Henri Nouwen also affirms the importance of creating space where meaningful questions can evolve. Writing to spiritual directors Nouwen says,

> To offer spiritual help requires, first of all, not to deny but to affirm the search. Painful questions must sometimes be raised, faced and then lived. This means that we must constantly avoid the temptation of offering or accepting simple answers, to be easy defenders of God, the Church, the tradition, or whatever else we feel we must defend.

Most of us are rescuers by nature. We would much rather help a person out of their quandary than help them stay in it. But that's exactly what spiritual direction does. It encourages a person to trust God in the very tensions that our questions raise, and to not prematurely resolve those tensions with easy answers. As Nouwen observes,

> The questions that lead us to seek spiritual direction are not questions with easy answers but ones that lead us deeper into the mystery of existence. What needs affirmation is the validity of these questions. What needs to be said is: "Yes, these are indeed the right questions. Don't be afraid to enter them. Don't turn away from living them. Don't worry if you don't have an immediate answer for them"

Spiritual direction affirms our basic quest for meaning. It calls for the creation of space where a more profound seeking can take place. By its very nature spiritual direction is "mystagogical"—it helps us see ourselves and all of life as a mystery that we are growing towards. Because it anticipates discovery it ensures that we are always growing in the spiritual life.

Spiritual direction helps open doors to new perspectives and horizons. It offers genuine hope that behind the difficult questions we will find, perhaps not the answers, but a deepening relationship to faith. As Nouwen puts it,

> We must allow all the daily experiences of life—joy, loneliness, fear, anxiety, insecurity, doubt, ignorance, the need for affection, support, understanding, and the long cry for love—to be recognized as an essential part of the spiritual quest. When we realize that the pain of the human search is a necessary part of growth, we can accept as good the forces of human spiritual development that our questions raise in us.

As we mature our questions, of course, will cease. Not because we have found the answers, but because we have come to more fully trust God with the things we cannot understand. Nouwen recognizes the purifying of our faith that this implies, when he writes,

> To receive spiritual direction is to recognize that God does not necessarily solve our problems or answer all our questions, but leads us closer to the mystery of our existence where all questions cease. It calls for the courage to enter into the common search and to confront the brokenness that begets our questions. It helps us accept that our questions are human questions, that our search is a human search, and that our restlessness is part of the restlessness of the human heart.

Spiritual direction then is mostly concerned with the formation of faith—our increasing capacity to welcome God as the mysterious Creator of our lives. It fosters a disposition in us that can only be sustained by prayer and it cultivates spiritual disciplines that invite us to slow down and order our time, our desires and our thoughts in such a way that we are more open to the mystery of God, before whom all questions cease.

35

Suddenly a furious storm came up on the lake, so that the waves swept over the boat. But Jesus was sleeping. The disciples went and woke him, saying, "Lord, save us! We're going to drown!" He replied, "You of little faith, why are you so afraid?" Then he got up and rebuked the winds and the waves, and it was completely calm.

Matt. 8:24-26

One thing that should be obvious to anyone who reads this passage from Matthew is that the Lord would've preferred to be left sleeping rather than awakened by the disciples' panicked response to bad weather. How does Jesus' preference also apply to our own fearful response to life? When Jesus seems asleep in the midst of our storms how do our own anxious prayers reveal the "little faith" we have?

It's certainly understandable that we want Jesus to "wake up" whenever we are afraid. But perhaps the Lord, secure in the knowledge that there really isn't a problem here, would prefer to have us rest in His peace rather than project our fears unto Him. It honours Jesus more when we trust that He is guiding us rather than presume He is asleep at the wheel.

How we respond to a crisis reveals a lot about our faith. The way we pray at such times can communicate more to God about our distrust than about our faith. Is it really a prayer of faith we are offering or is it a prayer of fear. Too often we interpret the seeming absence or reticence of the Lord as abandonment. But, in faith, we could just as easily interpret this as a reassuring sign of Jesus' confidence that there really isn't a problem here.

The next time we are in crisis, rather than immediately cry for help, perhaps it would be good to ask ourselves what an alternative prayer of faith might look like in this situation. Such a prayer would probably sound less like that of the disciples in the boat and more like the prayers of the Psalmists who, in the midst of their own trials, found the confidence to assert that,

> God is our refuge and strength,
> an ever-present help in trouble.
> Therefore we will not fear, though the earth give way
> and the mountains fall into the heart of the sea. (Psalm 46:1-2)

We honour God most by trusting Him—in other words, by being so assured of His care that we are even willing to let Jesus sleep. The story of the disciples in the storm highlights the fact that God hears not only our prayers but also the motivation behind them. Even when we think we are disguising our anxieties in the form of a prayer, our lack of faith is nevertheless evident to God.

36

As we have heard, so we have seen.

Psalm 48:8

Most of our understandings of God come from the theologies we have been taught. This, of course, is an essential part of our spiritual formation. But one of the problems with a spirituality that begins in the mind is that it often stays there. We end up knowing much more *about* God than we have ever actually experienced.

Most of us, for instance, are well schooled in the theology and belief that the Lord is good. We are also taught, from an early age, that God is faithful, merciful and loving. But, for many Christians, these are truths that have been "heard" but not necessarily "seen."

To truly "know" God means to have first-hand experience of His character—a knowledge that can only come from walking closely with the Lord in all aspects of our life. It would be fair to say that only a person who has had to trust God in the dire straits of life has truly experienced the assurance of God's faithfulness. Only those who have approached the Lord in the vulnerability of their own brokenness can know, first-hand, how God loves them just as they are. And only the sinner who has recognized God's sovereign right to judge us can fully appreciate the saving mercy of Christ that our theology speaks of.

To their dismay many people discover during times of crisis, that a belief system, on its own, is not enough to anchor them in their faith. What they need at such times is not so much a right understanding, but a true knowledge of the character of God who is standing with them in their trials.

A first-hand knowledge of God is the most important thing we can pursue in this life, and now is the given time to cultivate such knowledge. It will be too late to come to terms with how we feel about the trustworthiness of God when we are in a panic, or in the confusing grip of fear.

The fact that God is good, loving, faithful, and that He provides for His children is something we have all been taught to believe. But how securely do we rest in these truths? In what ways has this knowledge been confirmed in our hearts? And to what degree can we say, as the Psalmist does, "As we have heard, so we have seen?"

37

"They worshipped and served the creature more than the creator."

Rom. 1:25

It was St. Augustine who first used the phrase *incurvatus in se* to describe the nature and spiritual direction of sin. He pictured the fundamental ailment of the human person as being *curvatus in se* ("being turned in upon oneself"). Martin Luther also used this expression in his *Lectures on Romans* describing our condition as *homo incurvatus in se*, that is, "humans curved in on ourselves." He wrote,

> Our nature, by the corruption of the first sin, is so deeply curved in on itself that it not only bends the best gifts of God towards itself, but it also fails to realize that it continually seeks all things, even God, for its own sake.

The phrase '*incurvatus in se*' shows up as well in a number of Luther's other writings. He uses it often to describe what he calls the inordinate "prudence of the flesh," saying,

> The prudence of the flesh chooses what is good for oneself and

avoids what is disadvantageous for oneself, and in so doing it often rejects the common good and what is good for community in favour of what best serves its own need. This idolatrous prudence directs our self-will to look out for itself and its own interests above all other matters.

Like those who believed the earth to be the center of the universe, so sin deceives us into thinking that all things revolve around our own needs, including God. Luther adds,

> This prudence makes man feel that he himself is the final and ultimate object in life. He considers good only those things which are for his own personal good, and those things only as evils which are bad for him.

So profound is this tendency to 'curve in on ourselves' that, without God's grace, it is not only incurable but also unrecognizable. Which is why the Lord is so intent on bringing this fatal characteristic to our attention, and on providing for its cure. Nor should it surprise us that the obvious remedy to being 'curved upon ourselves' is to become more curved upon others. As Luther writes,

> You are completely curved in upon yourself and pointed toward love of yourself, a condition from which you will not be delivered unless you learn to love your neighbour more than yourself. For it is a perversity to overly want to be loved by all and to seek our own interests in all people. But it is uprightness if you do to everyone else what you want done to yourself.

Paul tells us as much in Phil. 2:3—that we should pay more attention to others than to ourselves, valuing them not only for what they represent to our "selfish ambition," but more for the ways we might bless them with our own lives. This same principle also applies to our relationship with God. Rather than being curvatus in se, the Holy Spirit is encouraging us towards a life that is more curvatus in Deo, in other words, more "curved upon God" than upon ourselves.

> *Do nothing out of selfish ambition or vain conceit. Rather, in humility value others above yourselves.*
>
> Phil. 2:3

38

The great dragon was hurled down—that ancient serpent
called the devil, or Satan, who leads the whole world astray.
He was hurled to the earth, and his angels with him.

Rev. 12:9

If Augustine was right in defining sin as *curvatus in se* (being turned in upon oneself), then Dante's depiction of Satan is a perfect symbol of the soul stuck in the cold despair of self-absorption. In the author's epic poem, *Inferno*, Hell is divided into nine circles, where the ninth circle is reserved for the worst sinners. Contrary to the popular images of Hell as a fiery place, sinners, in Dante's allegory, are actually frozen in a lake of ice. Satan himself sits in this last ring, trapped waist-deep in the ice.

For Dante, the epitome of Hell is the complete separation of our souls from the light and warmth of life. Satan himself conveys the ultimate pain of Hell, which is total isolation and self-absorption. Virgil, who is Dante's guide, explains to the author, "the inhabitants of the infernal region are those who have lost their capacity to discern evil, which results in the loss of their humanity, good will, and their capacity to love."

In Dante's *Inferno*, Satan is a much less powerful figure than we see in most depictions. Stuck in the ice, he weeps and beats his wings as if trying to escape. Ironically, it is the very flapping of his wings that generates the wind that keeps the lake frozen. If he stopped beating his wings the ice would melt and he could be free. But in order to escape, Satan would have to fly, which would again freeze the water and trap him in the ice. It is the paradox of God's judgment that the very wings which Satan thinks are the means of his escape, are actually the cause of his "chains."

Having plumbed the depths of Hell, Virgil tells Dante that they must now return to earth, which they do in a remarkable way. Carrying Dante on his back, Virgil approaches Satan and starts climbing onto his giant body. Gripping the Devil's frozen tufts of hair he then lowers himself and his companion down, below Lucifer's waist, and through the ice itself. Once beneath the frozen lake, they reach Satan's submerged legs, and here Virgil slowly turns himself around, and starts climbing upward. Dante is startled by the fact that Lucifer's legs now rise above them until Virgil explains that when Satan fell from Heaven, he plunged headfirst into the planet; his body stuck here in the center. In other words, Hell is an upside-down version of all that life should be.

There is much profound symbolism in Dante's *Inferno* regarding the nature and effects of sin. Sin is understood as a process of increasing self-absorption which ultimately leads us away from the warmth of life. And the entrapment of sin is that it keeps us perpetually preoccupied with ourselves as we desperately try to fix, or save, our own lives.

Dante's vision is quite different from the imagery of Hell we are used to. Perhaps this short summary of a Renaissance classic might provide opportunity to meditate on our own spiritual direction as we sense God calling us away from the dangerous isolation of self-absorption, and more towards the warmth of His love, and of our love for others.

39

Seek first the kingdom of God and all these things shall be added to you.

Matt. 6:33

Much thought and energy goes into the important task of teaching good theology in our churches. The assumption is that, if people have a right understanding of faith, they will automatically know what to do with it. But we often see just the opposite. Many Christians, though steeped in the good teaching of the church, are nevertheless lukewarm in their faith and cold in their desires for more of God.

Such hearts need a particular type of pastoral encouragement. They need to be reminded often of their first love, and given hope that there are tangible ways to draw near to God and to cultivate the spiritual life they wish to have. Sadly, these are the very teachings that often seem to be missing in many of our churches' curriculum. In this observation, I am in the good company of Jeanne Guyon who lamented a similar lack of spirituality in her own day (18th cent.), and its consequences for the church's outreach. She writes,

> O how inexpressibly great is the loss sustained by the Church from the neglect of the Interior Life! If all who laboured for the conversion of others were to introduce them immediately into

Prayer and the Interior Life and make it their main design to gain and win over the heart, numberless as well as permanent conversions would certainly ensue.

We often feel dismayed by the church's declining status in our day. We witness not only disinterest from those outside the church, but also a worrisome sense of apathy from those within. Why is this? Guyon offers a wise diagnosis saying,

The cause of our being so unsuccessful in reforming mankind is our beginning with external matters. Our labours in this field cannot, on their own, produce fruit that endures: but if the key of the interior life be first given, the exterior would be naturally and easily reformed.

In her desire to teach others how to seek and find God in their own lives Guyon represents something of the same mission we feel called to with Imago Dei. She writes,

To teach someone to seek God in their heart, to return to Him whenever they find they have wandered, and to do all things with a single eye to please Him is the natural and ready process that leads the soul to the very source of Grace, wherein is to be found all that is necessary for sanctification.

Guyon concludes with an exhortation to church leaders, and especially to pastors—that they focus their attention on the hearts of their congregants, and encourage them to continually submit their lives to the reign of Christ. She writes,

O ye dispensers of His grace, ye preachers of His Word, ye ministers of His Sacraments, establish His kingdom! And that it may indeed be established, make Him ruler over the hearts of His subjects! For as it is the heart alone that can oppose His Sovereignty, it is by the subjection of the heart that His Sovereignty is most highly exalted.

It would be hard to disagree with Guyon's conclusion that, since such submission is the goal of our faith, it should also be at the forefront of our teaching. May God's kingdom rule in the hearts of all. And may it increasingly be so with us.

40

Jesus made the disciples get into the boat and go on ahead of him to the other side, while he dismissed the crowd. After he had dismissed them, he went up on a mountainside by himself to pray. Later that night, he was there alone, and the boat was already a considerable distance from land, buffeted by the waves because the wind was against it. Shortly before dawn Jesus went out to them, walking on the lake. When the disciples saw him walking on the lake, they were terrified. "It's a ghost," they said, and cried out in fear. But Jesus immediately said to them: "Take courage. It is I. Don't be afraid." "Lord, if it's you," Peter replied, "tell me to come to you on the water."

"Come," he said.

Mat. 14:22-28

Sometimes it's hard to tell if the spirit who is calling us in a certain direction is really Jesus or not. Like the disciples in the boat, we can't always be sure what it is we're seeing on the horizon. It might be Jesus who is walking towards us on the water, but it could just as easily be a ghost. And we certainly risk foolishness if we get out of the boat too soon and try walking on the water only to find that it wasn't Jesus after all. But it can be just as foolish to remain stuck in our doubts—to feel we need to absolute proof before we can move.

Perhaps Peter's response is best. While the rest of the disciples hesitate in fear because they aren't sure what is out there, Peter puts this uncertainty to a simple test: "Lord, if it's you," he says, "tell me to come to you on the water." It is a wonderful method that applies to the many ambiguities we often face in our discernment.

Consider your sense of being "stuck" between two options as similar to the disciples' experience of rowing against the wind throughout the night. We are trying to discern God's will but we're getting nowhere. Then, suddenly, we see the faint hint of what might be Jesus walking towards us, but we're not sure. It could also be a ghost.

With such little information to go on we're not sure if we should move or stay put. And so we simply ask the only Person who can verify God's presence to us, "Is that really You I am seeing Lord? And, if so, would you call me to walk on the water with You?"

Discernment is not simply a matter of asking whether the winds are favourable, or whether the water can support us. It is concerned mostly with the question of whether or not the voice we are hearing is truly Jesus'. Like Peter, we should let Jesus confirm the validity of His presence before we set out in a particular direction. If we sense the Lord inviting us, it is simply a matter of finding the faith to follow Him onto the waters of uncertainty. But if the Lord does not confirm His presence to us, then we are best to stay in the boat—to keep rowing against the prevailing winds until we are more certain who is calling us to this direction or decision.

41

Do I bring to the moment of birth and not give delivery?"
says the Lord

Isa. 66:9

The end of any discernment process will naturally presume some action on our part. That's why discernment can be understood as "prayer meeting action." In other words, the final stage of any discernment process will inevitably require of us the courage to act.

But the process of discernment can sometimes lead to a place of paralysis where a person cannot, or perhaps *will* not, choose a course of action out of fear of being wrong. They have done all the preliminary prayer work of discernment. They have established impartiality in themselves, remaining at an equilibrium regarding all the options before them. They have removed from themselves the influence of inordinate desires or fears that would bias their decision, and they have given their wills over to God's pleasure as best they can. But in the process of being so open-handed in their disposition, they have perhaps also relinquished their will to act.

We often have a pretty good idea of what God is calling us to do. But, consciously or subconsciously, we also delay the inevitable action that this choice will require of us. Feeling stuck like this—unable to bring to birth that which we have conceived—reveals an underlying disposition that is important to acknowledge in the discernment process. It is the fear of facing the onerous responsibility of making a choice. Through our inaction, we are in fact saying to God, "I don't really want to make this decision. I want You to make it for me." But this is where God turns the tables on us. If we have been saying to the Lord, "I want whatever You want," the Lord now says to us, "Good, but you must now choose what you think I want."

As discerning Christians we are to assume the responsibility of not only seeking God's will in our lives but of also acting in the world according to that discernment. In the freedom of faith, it is up to us to choose, with God's counsel, how to best serve Him. And it is a shirking of that responsibility when our discernment process simply ends with the prayer, "You decide for me."

Fear of making a choice can keep us paralyzed in an unfruitful state of discernment. This is the image the Lord gives in Isaiah 66:9—of a baby stuck in the labour process. Discernment is never a substitute for faith. Nor is it an excuse to dump our hard decisions on God. But it does take courage—the final thrust of faith—to bring to birth that which we have conceived in our discernment, and to counter the paralyzing fear that sometimes sabotages the process of "prayer meeting action."

42

If your eye be single your whole body will also be full of light.

Luke 11:34

I was on a retreat once where we were each given a lump of self-hardening clay. We were asked to create an image with the clay that would depict our deepest desire for this time away with Jesus. I had no trouble knowing what I was going to make with this clay as a particular image had long been forming in me as I prepared for this retreat. I was looking forward, above all, to a time of focusing where Jesus might draw my attention away from all the things that were distracting me, and bring me more single-mindedly to Himself. I had often pictured this in the image of a funnel as I looked forward to offering myself in this way to the Lord—that He would gather me from the width and breadth of the many expressions of my life and bring me into a single point of focus on Him.

I set out to create the funnel by first rolling the clay on a table until I ended up with one long, thin string. I then made a large paper funnel out of construction paper, taped it, and slowly started spiraling the clay string inside the paper funnel. Eventually, the clay hardened and I removed the construction paper. I was pleased to see a pretty good representation of the image I had been praying. As I looked into the wide end of the funnel, I imagined myself entering and being gathered in from all sides towards God who awaited me at the small end of the funnel.

We were then asked to place our clay sculptures on the floor before the altar and to consider how the Lord might wish to respond to these prayers. I was surprised at what God showed me of His related desire for me in through this symbol. As I looked at my funnel from the other way around, from the small end to the mouth, I recognized it as a cornucopia—a place from which the bounty of a harvest comes flowing forth. I now saw the clay sculpture from both sides—from my perspective, as the narrowing of my self towards God, and from His, as the bounty of life He then produces in us from this simple offering.

Jesus invites us to "lose ourselves" in Him—to allow Him to become the increasing focus of our lives. And He also promises to all who respond to this invitation an abundance of life. It is a glorious and gracious exchange. In giving up the width and breadth of my complex existence, and bringing my focus to a single point on Jesus, far from losing life, I end up gaining passage, through the narrow gate, to the increasing glory of a life lived more singly with God.

43

I have learned to be content whatever the circumstances. I know what it is to be in need, and I know what it is to have plenty. I have learned the secret of being content in any and every situation, whether well fed or hungry, whether living in plenty or in want.

Phil 4:11-12

Tucked away between the second and third weeks of St. Ignatius' *Spiritual Exercises* is a short meditation which he calls "The Three Classes of Men." It speaks of the various degrees of attachment we can find ourselves in with regards to things that we know God would rather us hold more loosely.

Ignatius invites us to imagine three men, each of whom has been given ten thousand ducats. This gift however is recognized by each of these men as an impediment to a genuinely free relationship with God, and they wish to rid themselves of the burden that this attachment is causing them. Though Ignatius uses money as the object of their attachment, his meditation naturally applies to any attachment we sense might be impeding our freedom with God.

The first man knows that the money he has been given represents an unhealthy attachment and he immediately wants to do something about it in order to find peace again with God. He plans to get rid of the money but he keeps putting it off. Unfortunately this first story ends abruptly as the man dies before he has done anything to rid himself of his attachment. Ignatius challenges us to ask ourselves about similar attachments in our own lives that we know God is calling us to deal with, but that we have been putting off.

The second man also recognizes the inordinate attachment he has to this money, and he too wants to do something about it. He wants however to deal with it in such a way that he will not necessarily lose the money in question. He rationalizes to himself that the problem is not really the money, but more the attachment that he has to it. Sound familiar? He has already decided that he wants to keep the money and now sets to work on dealing solely with the problem of his attachment. This man represents those who, in Ignatius' words, "want to rid themselves only of the discomfort of their attachment, while still retaining the object of their attachment."

The third man is the only one who truly detaches himself from the money. His objective is not necessarily to get rid of it, but to assume that it is already forfeit. Ignatius identifies such people as those who are able to rid themselves of their attachments in such a way that "they desire neither to retain nor to relinquish the sum acquired." They seek rather whatever is best for the service and praise of their Lord. In the meantime they act as though "every attachment to it has been broken." As far as they are concerned, the money is no longer theirs. As a result, their attention is not fixed on trying to free themselves from their attachment nor from the discomfort they feel regarding their attachment. It is now solely focused on what Ignatius calls the "holy indifference" that best serves God.

Ignatius' allegory highlights how easy it is to deceive ourselves about the things we are attached to, and how difficult it is to truly be "indifferent" with regards to things that really matter to us. As you imagine yourself in the shoes of each of these "classes of men" perhaps you will recognize your own attachment to things that confuse your freedom with God. Is it money? Work? Time? People? Your health? What is your attachment and how have you tried (or not) to be free of it? Have you seen yourself procrastinating until you never get around to what you know God is calling you to deal with? Have you tried to deal solely with the discomfort your attachment is causing you rather than deal with the object of your attachment itself? Or are you truly free of both the problem as well as the desire that your attachment represents to you? These are the questions that Ignatius challenges us with. They represent as well the very invitation towards the freedom of life that Jesus wishes us to have.

44

Seek first the kingdom of God and his righteousness.

Mat. 6:33

We generally think of righteousness in terms of our relationship to morality or to people. But the word means much more than that. It means to be rightly related to all things in your life—to exercise, to sleep, to your diet, to your finances, to work, to ministry, to your possessions, to entertainment. These are all areas where righteousness applies. And they are also areas where we often feel off-kilter. We keep trying to find a balance, but we keep missing the mark.

God is always indicating to us adjustments we need to make in life, which is why we should approach righteousness more as an act of obedience than one of discipline or self- management. If we simply heed the correctives of the Holy Spirit, God is prepared to show us how to live without excess or neglect in our relationship to all things.

Peace and stability are generally the indicators of being rightly related to something. In the OT, when righteousness prevailed, the people enjoyed *shalom*, a word that speaks of wholeness, rest, harmony, and of the absence of agitation or discord. When everything is in right relationship to everything else, the result is *shalom*.

Turmoil, on the other hand, usually indicates adjustments are still needed. It creates tension in us until the changes that life is crying out for are made. Such restlessness is a God-given instinct through which the Holy Spirit teaches us the correctives we need. Just as our inner ear can tell us when we are standing off balance, so this God-given instinct helps us recognize when there is imbalance in any of our relationships. If we simply follow its leading, the Holy Spirit will free us from all the unnecessary turmoil that being wrongly related to something produces in our lives.

The Holy Spirit's correctives will nag us until we either do something about them or else shut them out. If we consistently ignore these promptings we will develop what Jesus calls a "calloused heart," which is not much different from the calluses we develop on our hands from manual labour, or on our feet from walking. Our bodies warn us when a blister is developing. It even provides pain to alert us of impeding injury. But if our inattentiveness persists, these repeated blisters eventually become a callus. Having refused to heed its first warnings, our body shifts to plan B. It hardens the skin, making itself insensitive to further stimulus. This is also what happens when we ignore the Holy Spirit's promptings. We end up losing our relational sensitivity to that area of our lives.

To seek and find righteousness in all our relationships is a realistic goal for any of us. We were created for righteousness in all areas of our life. We simply need be more attentive to the discords we sense, to recognize them for what they are—the promptings of the Holy Spirit—and to obey whatever adjustments they are calling for.

45

"Fill it to the brim..."

John 2:7

The party has begun, but the wine has already run out. The stores are closed and there is no backup plan. Humanly speaking there is nothing that can be done to avert the embarrassing situation that is about to unfold. But Mary reaches out into the impossible. She talks to Jesus. Though He replies that His hour has not yet arrived, Mary has a mother's hunch that it will not be long in coming. She instructs the servants to "do whatever He tells you to do." And, of course, the rest is history. They fill the urns with water, and Jesus tops up their minimal efforts with His abundant grace.

How does this same invitation apply in my own life, whenever I feel I have come to the end of my resources? My deficiencies are exposed and there is nothing I can do about it. I have no reserves in myself to be the person I want to be. Humanly speaking, there is nothing I can do to avert the embarrassment of being exposed as the poor Christian I truly am. But I reach out into the impossible. I tell Jesus. It might not yet be the hour of my release but faith tells me that it will not be long in coming.

Jesus instructs the servants to, "Take the water urn and fill it to the brim." He tells me similarly, "Do whatever, humanly speaking, you can." And so I present myself to Him in my impoverished state and do all I can to "fill the urn to the brim." This is my offering—to give to the Lord whatever I have of the raw materials of my life to work with. It's not quite the choice wine that I had in mind, but it's the best I can do with what is at hand.

The servants do as they are instructed. Then Jesus tells them to, "draw from the urn and bring it to the chief steward." He says similarly to me, "Now go and act on what you have." Both Jesus and I both know that there is nothing more than water in these urns, but I serve it to the guests anyhow.

As the servants obey Jesus, they are amazed at what comes pouring out of their ladles. Not only has the water changed into wine but the quality of this final offering far exceeds that of the first wine served. I too, acting in faith, am equally amazed at how Jesus tops up my offering in ways that far exceed the quality of my own feeble efforts.

The Lord's first miracle at Cana has many applications for us whenever we too have "run out of wine"—when we encounter the truth of our own poverty of spirit. At such times, as this story counsels, we must first accept the reality of what is. The wine vat is truly empty. There is no need to deny it, nor to conceal this fact from others. Then, like Mary, we come to Jesus and talk with Him about our "impossible" situation—what seems beyond our human capabilities at the moment.

But before we presume to dump our problem on Jesus, it is only right that we first do whatever we can to fill our own efforts to the brim. In other words, in spite of what might seem impossible, we should never lose hope for what the Lord can do when He adds His grace to our own meager initiatives.

46

Then the eyes of both of them were opened, and they
realized they were naked; so they sewed fig leaves together
and made coverings for themselves. Then the man and his
wife heard the sound of the Lord God as he was walking in
the garden in the cool of the day, and they hid from the Lord
God among the trees of the garden.

Gen. 3:7-9

Adam and Eve never actually repented for their disobedience. They tried instead to manage their sins, covering themselves with fig leaves, and hiding their self-perceived shame from each other. They also hid from God. Even when confronted with their transgression, they looked for excuses rather than repent. They blamed each other, twisting the truth in the hope of deflecting God's gaze. Sound familiar? It should. For we too, often opt for such alternatives to simply repenting.

Repentance is not usually our first recourse when confronted with sin. Our more immediate instinct is to want to hide from God, from others, and from ourselves. And when that doesn't work we then try to manage our sins. Rather than simply come to God, we try instead to save and heal ourselves.

There are iniquities in my life that I have been trying to deal with for years. I have often prayed about these, seeking God's help and healing. Many times I have asked God for the strength to change, or for more willpower in these areas of my life. But have I ever simply asked the Lord for a more genuine spirit of repentance with regards to these sins? Have I ever truly repented for these sins? Or have I too quickly bypassed this step by assuming for myself the task of self-repair?

Genuine repentance begins and ends with God. The Lord Himself had to introduce the concept of repentance to us through the institution of the Tabernacle and the sacrifices He prescribed for sin. Like children, we had to be taught how to recognize and acknowledge our transgressions. We had to name our sins, to own them, and to confess them. God Himself had to show us how to make restitution, and how to trust Him for the forgiveness and restoration we need. And God continues to teach us today, through the conviction of the Holy Spirit, the path that leads from repentance to forgiveness.

What we require most for our sanctification is a truer spirit of repentance. Rather than trying to change ourselves, or manage our sins on our own, we should simply ask God to give us a more genuine spirit of repentance—true sorrow, even tears—regarding the things we regret in our lives. It is, by far, the most direct way to be reconciled to God.

47

Blessed are those who mourn, for they will be comforted.

Matt. 5:4

Many spiritual traditions place a high value on the role of grief and mourning in facilitating both personal and communal transformation. Ancient Christian monasticism gives particular attention to how tears open up the soul, creating the possibility of a more authentic relationship to God and to others. Douglas E. Christie, in his book, *The Blue Sapphire of the Mind,* speaks of the Christian monks of the fourth century who believed that the "gift of tears" helped awaken the soul to the reality of life. He writes.

> Tears, in the ancient Christian monastic world, were believed to express and make possible an honest reckoning with one's life (especially one's fragility). They were the catalyst for life-changing transformation; a reorientation to God and to the larger community.

Though we cannot fabricate such tears, we can seek and welcome them as a precious gift from God, given to help us deepen our capacity for seeing, feeling, and responding to the world and to the movements of our own soul. Christie recognizes the personal edification that such tears provide when he writes,

> The early Christian monks spoke of being "pierced" to the depth of their souls, and of tears flowing in a moment of sudden recognition of an aspect of their own moral-spiritual life that was in need of healing or renewal. The tears themselves became the means of that healing, the medium through which a clearer, more honest awareness of oneself, the world and God became possible.

To be moved to tears by a heart-piercing recognition of our bondage to sin and of its consequent effects on those around us was a sign of mature faith for these early Christians. Christie writes of the redemptive effects of such heart-felt responses saying,

> The piercing recognition of one's helplessness in the face of the debilitating habits of sloth or greed or pride or anger sometimes yielded a sense of release expressed in tears, whose healing power no amount of conscious reflection could ever hope to match. Tears, through the sheer force with which they moved through one's being, became a primary means through which one could be brought to face our bondage to sin and be adequately motivated to seek release from it.

The early Christian monks welcomed tears as a means of breaking open the soul because they recognized how important it was to feel grief in the face of loss and brokenness. They also saw the inability to weep as something to be taken very seriously. As Christie writes,

> It is possible to ignore or refuse to acknowledge the truth of our brokenness. But doing so means relinquishing oneself to a kind of moral and spiritual blindness, an existence characterized by little possibility for intimacy or reciprocity with others. Hence the need to ask oneself continuously: am I capable of tears? Am I capable of opening myself to the beauty and pain of my own soul, of the souls of others and of the world itself?

Our hearts do not always respond to life as they should, and to confess this represents the beginning of genuine hope for the regeneration of this faculty in ourselves. It is the likely prerequisite for being blessed with the "gift of tears."

48

> *As Jesus and his disciples, together with a large crowd, were leaving the city, a blind man, Bartimaeus, was sitting by the roadside begging. When he heard that it was Jesus of Nazareth, he began to shout, "Jesus, Son of David, have mercy on me!" Many rebuked him and told him to be quiet, but he shouted all the more, "Son of David, have mercy on me!"*
>
> Mark 10:46-48

Perhaps you too have cried out at times what might be called a "shot in the dark" prayer—those prayers we make to the walls and ceiling in the hope that there is a God out there who just might hear us. Bartimaeus, the beggar from Jericho, certainly exemplifies such faith and the blind hope (in his case literally) that reaches out for God in spite of our doubts.

Bartimaeus is used to calling out in the dark for what he needs. He is a beggar after all, and blind to boot. Sitting by the roadside, with only the sound of footsteps to go on, he spends his day calling out to passersby, trying to draw attention to himself. So why should today be any different?

The blind man hears a crowd going by. "What's happening," he shouts to anyone within earshot. "It's Jesus of Nazareth," a woman replies as she walks past the beggar. Bartimaeus spends a lot of time listening to the conversations that surround his dark world. He's heard of Jesus before. And he knows that this man apparently heals people. What's there to lose?

"Jesus, Son of David, have mercy on me," he yells above the din of the crowd. He is just one of many voices in the confusion of people that surround Jesus, but Bartimaeus, more than anyone, knows how to make himself heard. He lets out another plaintive and well-rehearsed cry that cuts through the otherwise civil discourse of others. "Have mercy on me," he shouts in the most poignant tone he can muster. Those closest to him certainly hear him, and their response is a familiar one to Bartimaeus. They want to quell this overly opportunist beggar. But, to everyone's surprise, the first miracle happens. Jesus hears his cry.

The crowd hushes as the Lord suddenly stops and says, "Call him to me." Anticipation rises. Something is about to happen here. Bartimaeus is not sure what is going on. And he is more surprised than anyone when, instead of trying to shut him up, he hears someone from the crowd actually calling him to come to the Master. "Cheer up," the voice says, "On your feet! He's calling you."

Bartimaeus doesn't waste a second. A beggar man knows just how fickle people's generosity can be. He jumps to his feet and lets himself be led a short distance. Then he hears a voice that asks what seems like a most rhetorical question, "What do you want me to do for you?" No introduction is needed. He knows who this is, and he replies in the most simple terms, "Rabbi, I want to see." Jesus responds with an equally direct pronouncement, "Go, your faith has healed you."

Bartimaeus has his reward. He, who only moments ago, from his dark and lonely world, had enough faith to at least try a blind shot in the dark, can now see. Everything has changed for him because of a little gumption on his part—the type of chutzpah that has sometimes worked for him in the past, but never as successfully as it has on this day.

Bartimaeus will live a very different life than would have been his lot had he too soon disqualified himself from the abundant possibilities that lay just beyond his capacity to see. His experience of God will also be very different than had he chosen to obey the voices suggesting to him that such a close relationship was somehow inappropriate for him. Instead, as Scripture tells us, when those doubts were raised in him, Bartimaeus, in blind faith, simply shouted all the louder.

49

I have become all things to all people.

1Cor. 9:22

I have three children and, as a father, I can testify to the unique love I have in relation to each one of them. There is a particular way that I love my daughter that is different from the way I love anyone else in the world. I can say the same about my son. There is no one in the world who evokes that same love in me as he does. My other son as well inspires a one-of-a-kind response in my heart. Nor does this apply only to my children. I can say the same about the unique way I love my wife, my parents, my friends, etc.

I highlight this because our varied experiences of love within community can also help us understand the particular love that God has for each one of us. We each elicit from God a love that is original—a love that would not exist, even in God, if we did not exist. In other words, the Lord would never have known the particular love He has for you if you weren't there to love. His relationship with you is unique. And the love He feels for anyone else cannot substitute for the love God feels for you.

With each of my children I have also had opportunity to witness how the love I feel for them has evolved over time. I have to keep adjusting my relationship to them according to how they are changing in their lives. Each season of their lives calls me to be attentive, in new ways, to the person they are becoming. This, of course, also applies to all my long-term friends and relatives. In other words, the challenge we each face—to "be all things to all people"—is as myriad as the number of evolving relationships we have, and as ever-changing as there are seasons in life.

God, of course, is not limited in His capacities to love us. Nor does the Lord need to grow in His love. But it is easy to imagine, from our earthly experience, the countless delights that God must discover in His own heart as His relationship with you evolves. Like us, the Lord has to be all things to all people as we each represent a unique application of His love. And He too has to continually adjust His love for you according to the person you are becoming.

50

In Him all things hold together.

Col. 1:17

When my daughter was in elementary school she learned how to play the violin. And, faithful parents that we were, we dutifully attended all her concerts. I must admit that this was often an aesthetically painful experience for me. As a musician with a trained ear, the sounds I heard, to be honest, were not always the most soothing.

Anyone who has played the violin knows how temperamental an instrument it can be in terms of intonation. There are no frets or markers on the neck of the instrument. The precise place where one places their finger on the neck in order to produce the note is rather arbitrary, and this resulted in a particular phenomenon at these string concerts that I have never heard anywhere else.

Imagine a beginner's orchestra made up of thirty grade two violin students trying to play "Ode to Joy" in unison when each of their notes has a different intonation. Like an unruly swarm of bees, the out-of–tune mass of sound moves up and down the scale. This happens throughout the piece except for those few merciful notes when the melody demands an open string on the violin. At that point, (and for that one note only), the whole orchestra suddenly comes into tune. It is like that high school experiment where a magnet under a piece of paper suddenly draws all the random iron filings into an ordered shape. But the reprieve is over too soon. By the very next bar, the orchestra goes back to every note, in its own distinctive way, being out of tune.

This sonic phenomenon has been forever etched in my memory. It comes to mind whenever I feel scattered or dissipated in my life or relationships. I know that I am out of tune with myself or with those around me, and that my life is just following the notes in a rather arbitrary way. But I take comfort at these times knowing there is an open string below me that I can return to by simply taking my fingers off the neck of my life.

This image also comes to mind whenever I serve Communion. For here too, we, the Church throughout history and the world—who are largely out of tune with ourselves and with each other, suddenly find ourselves brought into order by the "magnet" that undergirds our faith. Through the historic act of remembering Christ in the bread and wine, we recover our intonation around the one true Note that gathers us all—the open string of Jesus' perfect pitch.

Like a violin, our lives, have no frets or markers to tell us where to put our fingers. There are, as a result, countless ways to be out of tune with ourselves and with each other. But thank God there is one place where we get to return to an intonation of unison—the very real presence of Jesus, in whom "all things hold together."

51

I am like a deaf man, who cannot hear, like a mute, who cannot open his mouth; I have become like a man who does not hear, whose mouth can offer no reply, I wait for You, O Lord; You will answer, O Lord my God.

Psalm 38:13-15

Most of us live in a fog when it comes to any real sense of God's presence in our lives. Like the Psalmist, we find ourselves more deaf and mute than we would like to be regarding the quality of our communication with the Lord. There are, of course, those rare and wonderful occasions when the clouds part and we experience a moment of clarity in this relationship. For the most part, like the Psalmist, we tend to see, hear and speak dimly.

Psalm 38 affirms this condition as normal. As the Psalmist confesses, "I am like a deaf man who cannot hear, like a mute, who cannot open his mouth." It might seem like a hopeless position from which to cultivate a relationship—like being in a foreign country where you cannot speak or understand the people you are trying to communicate with—if not for the faith that God understands our human predicament. Such is the confidence of the Psalmist. Rather than despair over his inability to pray, he offers the very condition of his lostness as the basis of his prayer.

Those rare times, when we once again know clarity in our communications with God are what provide faith for us that, if we simply keep returning to prayer, these times will surely return. Such is the Psalmist's hope when he says to God, "I will wait for you, O Lord, my God," and then adds the confident assurance that "You will answer, O Lord."

Maturity helps us accept the limitations of our creatureliness when it comes to initiating communications with God. But experience also teaches us that, if we wait long enough—if we persevere, and not give up on prayer—the Lord, in His time, will answer us. From His own gracious initiative, clarity will return to us. The fog will lift, the clouds will part, and the sun of truth will shine on us once again.

52

How long, Lord? Will you forget me forever?
How long will you hide your face from me?
How long must I wrestle with my thoughts
and day after day have sorrow in my heart?

Psalm 13:1-2

We do a disservice to others whenever we idealize prayer and only speak of it in glowing terms. What is needed is a more honest articulation of not only the sweetness of prayer but also its challenges—the ways we struggle with the flesh, and suffer long from the absence of what we desire most.

We often feel defeated when we cannot pray as we wish. It might be the busyness of our schedules that doesn't allow time for prayer. Or perhaps it's the busyness of our inner life that seems to block our access to God.

Even when we do sit down to pray, we often find ourselves unable to do so.

We can easily think that prayer has failed us at such times, and that we must resign ourselves to feeling distant from God. But something even more mysterious is going on in our hearts when we cannot pray than when we can, especially as we experience disappointment over this. A purification is taking place within the very longings that cause us to suffer the acute sense of loss we feel. The fact that we actually miss God and that we pine for a state of soul other than the one we are in is evidence of the vitality of our desire for God.

Love accentuates our experience of loss, for without love we would not care as much about the sense of separation we feel from God. We long to return to a quality of relationship that we have tasted and that has subsequently ruined us for anything less in life. It is because we have known such love that we yearn for its return. And this very longing for what has been lost is evidence of the Holy Spirit interceding for us through the wordless groanings of our heart.

Sometimes the most poignant prayer we can offer to God is the faint whisper that says, "I miss You." This is the prayer that is being purified in us when, for whatever reason, we are unable to pray as we would like to. From such a place of alienation our hearts cry out with sighs too deep for words: "How much longer Lord?"

The fact that it matters to you that you are unable to pray is a prayer in itself. Ironically, this very longing is what is being purified and perfected in you by the seeming problem of your inability to pray. It is a profound language of the heart that we need to become more familiar with—to know that the groaning of our spirits for "what we do not have" is, in itself, a sufficient prayer and not evidence for the lack of it.

53

Show me your ways, O Lord...teach me your truth.

Psalm 25:4

One thing Scripture stresses over and over again is the importance of seeking God's counsel in all we do. We are often told, for instance, to "wait upon the Lord" rather than act on our own. Such waiting represents a very slow and deliberate process of conversion—from our natural propensity to "lean on our own understanding" towards a life lived more in tandem with God in which we "acknowledge the Lord in all our ways" (Prov. 3:5-6).

The book of Proverbs also reminds us that there is "a way that seems right unto man" that actually destroys the sensitive life of our spiritual relationship (Prov. 16:25). And yet, admittedly, that is where the majority of our decisions come from—we simply do whatever we think is best. We are, of course, well-meaning in this and might be applying the best wisdom we can to the issues we face but we nevertheless make most of our decisions primarily on the basis of "what seems right" to *us*. A recurring rebuke in the OT is that Israel "did not seek the counsel of the Lord" (e.g. Josh. 9:14). Instead, as the book of Judges repeatedly states, "everyone did what was right in their own eyes" (e.g. Judges 21:25). Or as Isaiah famously puts it, "all we like sheep have gone astray; each of us has turned to our own way" (Isa. 53:6). How are we to avoid such charges in our own lives and submit more consistently to God's counsel in all we do?

Psalm 25 models for us the obvious corrective to such over-reliance on ourselves. It offers a simple prayer which, if we repeat daily, will train us to submit more consistently to God's higher ways in all aspects of our lives. It first acknowledges that we don't necessarily know God's ways nor what is best for us. From this more modest self-understanding, it then places us under the Lord's tutelage as we ask Him each day: "Show me *your* ways, O Lord, teach me *your* truth."

We are right to suspect that *our* ways and *our* truths are, at best, myopic and biased. In recognition of this, we choose the better wisdom of not overly leaning on our own understanding, even if it seems right in our own eyes. Instead, we wean ourselves from the over-confidence of our "adult" selves and learn to walk more securely in the healthy self-doubt of the children of God—those who daily look to their Creator, who alone knows how our lives should be lived.

54

For as in Adam all die, so in Christ all will be made alive.
1Cor. 15:22

There is a beautiful and theologically profound statue at the Chartres Cathedral in France that depicts a young man leaning on Christ's lap who, in turn, comforts him with a tenderness so exquisitely expressed by the artist that one cannot help but want to identify with the recipient of such caring love.

What story is being depicted here? What has happened before this scene that now elicits such consolation from our Lord? The young man seems exhausted, as though he has come a long way to find his rest. His posture is one of deep and humble gratitude. He seems to be holding onto Christ, not for supplication but for relief. His trial, whatever it has been, is finally over. He rests now, never again wanting to leave the company of His Saviour.

Who is this man that Christ consoles in such a particular way? Is it John, the disciple whom Jesus loved, who lays his head on Jesus' lap as he once did on the night the Lord was betrayed? Is it the prodigal son returning to the bosom of the Godhead, or the lost one for whom the Shepherd left the ninety-nine to find?

No, this is someone else, someone far more crucial to the story of

Redemption. For this man is Adam. Adam, who, from the first days of creation, bore, along with his wife, the guilt of disobedience that caused all of life to fall from grace. Adam, for whom no means of restitution was ever offered, for whom no sacrifice was available that would cleanse the blot of his original sin. Adam, who bears responsibility for the suffering and death of each of his offspring. Adam, who once enjoyed a life that was intimately united with God's—a human life without precedent nor ever to be repeated again. Adam, who has also known the horror of being exiled, seemingly forever, from the intimacy he was once favoured with.

Knowing who it is that is being comforted by Christ's initiative makes this scene all the more poignant. Adam has been redeemed! He has been restored to grace. "It is over," Jesus seems to be saying. "I have forgiven the guilt of your sin." "Behold, I make all things new again."

No wonder the young man rests so completely as he does in Jesus' caress. He has been released from the consequences of his trespass. He who introduced guilt to the whole human race, is now restored unto Christ. His sins, and ours, are washed away. And by the grace of Christ, after all these years, Adam can look once more at his soul and see it as he remembered it— as white as snow, innocent of all transgressions. It truly is a story of amazing grace!

55

Choose my instruction instead of silver,
knowledge rather than choice gold,
for wisdom is more precious than rubies,
and nothing you desire can compare with her.

Prov. 8:10-11

In his *Dark Night of the Soul,* St John of the Cross speaks of an ailment that particularly afflicts those who are adept at prayer—they become too attached to the consolations of prayer. It is a natural temptation related to the bliss of being near God that easily leads to what John of the Cross calls "spiritual gluttony." As he writes,

> The pleasures of the interior life become so great; they so far transcend the crude joys of sense and of this world, that they

exercise a terrible attraction upon the soul that meets them along its road to God.

What makes this attraction "terrible" is that we start presuming that the pleasure we feel in response to the presence of God is, in fact, God's presence. The danger, of course, is that we will just as easily interpret the absence of such feelings as indicating the absence of God's nearness. Until we are weaned from spiritual satisfaction as an end in itself, our feelings of bliss will falsely suggest that these, in themselves, are proof of God's nearness. It is no wonder that we end up with such an anxious relationship to the presence or absence of spiritual experience. As John of the Cross writes,

> The thought of these pleasures, the memory of them and the hope of their return move us to the very depths of our spirit with an inordinate desire for more. In our fear that they might never return we will do anything to bring back the joy we have once tasted in God's presence.

According to John of the Cross, someone in this condition has developed a "spiritual sweet tooth." Focusing on the temporary rewards of our own spiritual satisfaction we become distracted from the true goal of our prayer, which is unity with God. We covet instead those experiences of well-being and their increase as ends in themselves. As he writes elsewhere,

> The gluttony which they have developed for spiritual experience makes them continually go too far, so that they pass beyond the limits of moderation within which the virtues are acquired and in which they consist.

As delightful as our spiritual experiences might be, once their return becomes the prime focus of our prayer, they have gone "beyond the limits of moderation." We must never forget our first love. As Teresa of Avila wisely counseled her directees, "we must learn to seek the God of consolations, more than the consolations of God."

The impulse to seek spiritual gratification as an end in itself must be countered. As John of the Cross reminds us, the way to God is a way of emptiness (Phil. 2:7a). Pure faith does not require the evidence of reason, nor confirmations from the body to validate it. It stands alone. In the end, we learn to prefer what John of the Cross calls the "dark night"—the faith by which we trust that God's nearness, His love and His guidance are present, even in the absence of our experiencing such.

56

As for the saints who are in the land, they are the glorious ones in whom is my delight.

Psalm 16:3

There is a secret and intimate fellowship that people who pray have with each other which has more to do with instinct than familiarity. Whether it is an old friend or someone we have just met, we often recognize a "family resemblance" that can only be described as spiritual friendship. We note in their spirits something of our own deepest affinities.

The more we experience the effects of prayer in our own lives, the more we recognize these same traits in others. In their speech and behaviour we see a similar fruit to the one the Lord is cultivating in us. And in our conversation with them we find a repose that comes from the fact that we both share the same desire for a growing intimacy with God. How rare it is though to find such friends. And how few and far between are the opportunities we have to speak with others about our deepest spiritual hopes and longings.

For too long, the most profound aspects of our spiritual lives have been privatized. We rarely have opportunity to commune with others around these themes. Unless you belong to a Bible study group where personal disclosure is encouraged, or are fortunate enough to have a spiritually mature companion or a good spiritual director, there are few occasions in our church gatherings to hear from one another about the complex relationship we have with our souls. For many people, books are the closest we come to having someone articulate our deepest aspirations for the spiritual life. But books, on their own, can also accentuate our spiritual loneliness.

Where do we go to find such outlets for hearing and expressing the intricacies of our inner life? For myself it has been the various Imago Dei groups I have been a part of over the years that have given me opportunity to grow in the articulation of my faith. Our weekly meditations and follow-up questions provide a springboard for discussion through which I get to hear others express the deep truths of their inner life. Over the weeks, months and years of meeting together we learn a rich and growing vocabulary that helps us put the often abstract groanings of the soul into words. Hearing other people's relationship to this journey also helps counter the isolation we so often feel regarding the deep questions we have about our spiritual lives.

Paul told his friend Philemon to "be active in sharing your faith so that you will know every good thing you have received in Christ" (Philemon 1:6). This is the fruit I have seen cultivated among us over the years as people gather to share their experiences of faith. In finding expression for our inner life, we come to more fully appreciate all the good things we have received in Christ.

57

The steadfast love of the Lord never ceases;
his mercies never come to an end;
they are new every morning.

Lam. 3:22-23

The ocean laps against the shore. Each wave extends towards the land, then draws back into itself. Sometimes a small shell is caught in this action. With each passing wave it is drawn nearer to the sea. As the water recedes, the shell advances a few inches and then rests until the next wave.

But sometimes the shell gets lodged in the sand. For a time it remains stuck there. The waves continue to lap around it but it no longer advances. The waves however now have another objective. With each passing they are now working around the shell, drawing away the sand that is keeping it from advancing towards the ocean. Eventually, enough sand will be taken away and the shell will be free once again to respond to the draw of the waves.

Watching such a scene unfold at the beach I can easily recognize the similar action of God in my life. His waves of grace have often washed over my life, lapping on my shores and drawing me to return to my Father's house. Sometimes my return is thirty fold, sometimes sixty or even a hundred fold.

But often, like the sea shell, I too get stuck in the sands of life. Though God's waves continue to lap on my shore, I no longer respond to its draw. At such times I can easily feel like God has left me behind. But faith tells me that, in spite of my seeming lack of progress, His waves are nevertheless clearing the sand that prevents me from advancing towards His love. Though I might not notice it, each wave is helping remove the obstacles that keep me from responding as I should.

Eventually His grace will dislodge me from whatever is holding me back, and I will be free to respond once more to His presence. Such is the everlasting mercy of God—it is new every morning. Whether we feel free or stuck, we can be certain that His waves are always drawing us towards Himself, and that He is intent on removing every obstacle in our way.

> *Whether we are aware of it or not, at every moment of our existence we are encountering God, who is trying to catch our attention, trying to draw us into a reciprocal, conscious relationship.*
>
> -William A. Barry, SJ

58

How long must I wrestle with my thoughts.

Psalm 13:2

Often, when I teach on silent prayer, questions come up regarding our thoughts and how they keep getting in the way of our first intention of focusing on God. If nothing else, our attempts to pray reveal to us just how unruly our inner life really is. Like the person who thinks they are in good physical shape until they try running up a hill, we too become more aware of the inner disorder of our lives the moment we try to rest and be silent before God.

What can be done about our overly active thought life—what St. John of the Cross calls "the foxes that ruin the vineyard?" How can we calm and quiet the turmoil within us so that we can pray?

We cannot force our minds to stop thinking. But we can certainly grow in our love for God to the point where we prefer His presence over even our most interesting or pressing thoughts. For some people this comes quite naturally. But for most of us a conversion of the heart is necessary before we are enamoured enough with God to leave ourselves in the wings.

How can we speak of such a conversion? Sometimes a picture is worth a thousand words. Below are a few illustrations that might communicate a possible spiritual direction for us as we negotiate our relationship to our thoughts during prayer.

Our first objective in prayer, of course, is to be with God, which I've illustrated as a broken line. For although this is our intention, we have not yet established it.

This first intention however soon gets side-tracked by another objective, usually related to a thought that attracts us. We must recognize the deliberate choice we are making here—that we are choosing to follow this thought rather than to seek God. The illustration of our relationship to such thoughts is represented below as a solid line, for it is stronger than our desire for God.

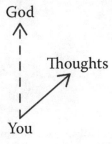

The question for us at this stage is not whether we are thinking or not, but whether we are alone with our thoughts. If we are alone, then we have left God and are no longer praying. But it is not always necessary to be alone with our thoughts. It is also possible to remain with God while we are thinking.

The moment we acknowledge God's awareness of our inner life our thoughts become a prayer, for we are no longer alone with ourselves. It can actually be very productive to go over the plans of your day with God, or perhaps your relationship to others, or to your circumstances. The next image illustrates this possibility.

God

Thoughts

You

Eventually though, and especially if you are praying for longer periods, you will start losing interest in your thoughts. God will become more attractive to you, and the grip that your thoughts have on you will start to loosen. As the next illustration suggests, the line of communication between you and God becomes more solid as the attraction to your thought life lessens.

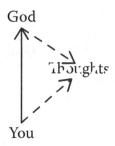

God

Thoughts

You

By the grace of the Holy Spirit, the final stage of this process will be the beauty of desiring nothing other than God. Our thoughts will no longer distract us as they did before. We have been weaned from their allure and are prepared now to rest in the sufficiency of God.

Having chosen God over all other attractions we are now content to remain in the Lord's presence. Our thoughts might still be active, but more in reflecting on the relationship we are now enjoying with God.

Words are no longer necessary at this stage of prayer as our communication becomes more of a wordless, spirit to Spirit dialogue. Our minds continue to observe and reflect on what is happening but there is really not much to say. We have chosen God over every other concern of the heart, and all else pales now compared to the simplicity of life we are enjoying with the Lord.

> *There are no words now, for our prayer moves beyond words.*
> *And yet there is a to-and-fro about it. He is calling us and we*
> *are following. God prays in us; it is His power and grace that*
> *help us pray, till we don't know where we leave off and He*
> *begins.*

Emily Griffin, *Clinging*

59

Everything exposed by the light becomes visible—and
everything that is illuminated becomes a light.

Eph. 5:13

Between 1980 and 1994, the frescoes of the Sistine Chapel, and in particular the ceiling and accompanying lunettes by Michelangelo, underwent a major restoration. The findings of an earlier investigation in 1979 revealed that the entire ceiling of the chapel was covered with a grime of candle smoke, wax and soot. Previous restorations had also left their marks on the frescoes where layers of varnish and glue that had been applied to many areas had darkened and become opaque, veiling the light's capacity to properly reflect the original colours. The final restoration revealed colours and details that had not been seen for centuries.

Lunette of "Daniel" (before and after restoration)

The concept of light being buried under the opaqueness of dirt is also a theme that Martin Laird explores in his book *Into the Silent Land* where he writes on the power of prayer to restore our original light. Lairds thesis is that, "Contemplative practice helps remove that which obscures the hidden self."

The idea that truth is not something that we have to aspire to but something that is already buried within us also resonates with Paul's teaching in 2Cor. 3:18 where he speaks of the glory we increasingly reflect the more we come to God with "unveiled faces." Laird too finds agreement with the apostle's imagery when he writes,

> The discipline of contemplation is not a technique but more of a surrendering of our deeply imbedded resistances. It allows the sacred within us to gradually reveal itself. Out of this letting go emerges what Paul calls our hidden self (Eph 3:16).

Jesus assures us that "the kingdom of heaven is within" (Luke 17:21). But we also know that there is much in our lives and in our self-understanding that obscures its light. Contemplative prayer helps remove these self-defining veils so that the Holy Spirit can lead us to the simple truth of our "unveiled" self—the purity of heart by which we come to see and reflect more truthfully our oneness with God (Mat. 5:8). This is what Laird suggests when he claims,

Union with God is not something that needs to be acquired as much as realized. Because of our unity with Christ, the reality of our oneness with God is already the case. The more we realize this to be true the more we can become ourselves just as we are.

Laird speaks of the foundational lie that veils and distorts our true self—that we tend to look to the creature for truth rather than to the Creator (Rom. 1:25). As a result of this misdirection of love we confuse our own dimly reflected light for God's Light, and we end up living a much different narrative than the one God intended for us.

We are caught between two worlds—our self-reflected identity and our God-reflected identity in Christ. Though we are in the process of being born again we still cling, in many ways, to the lies of our old, autonomous self. Laird speaks of animals who have lived most of their lives in cages who, once released into the wild, still live as if they were caged. They are free but they do not know it. This also mirrors our spiritual reality as Christians. We are free, but the memory of the cage still remains. This is why it is so important to come to God each day in prayer. If nothing else it reminds us over and over again of our essential unity with Christ.

"You *are* the light of the world," Jesus taught us. Our light is not something that lies ahead of us or that we must somehow become. It is actually hidden beneath us. We do not need to achieve or aspire to this reality as much as to simply rest in it. As we allow God's truth to reveal to us the simplicity of our creatureliness—of our lives as something received more than something we create—we too will be more fully illuminated by His light. "Everything exposed by the light will become visible," as Paul teaches. "And everything that is illuminated will itself become a light."

60

Do not be like the horse or the mule,
which have no understanding
but must be controlled by bit and bridle
or they will not come to you.

Psalm 32:9

What seems to honour God most in this life is when His children, who have the freedom to do whatever they wish, choose to orient their lives in His direction. It is also what most dignifies us as humans. This choice is perhaps most explicit when we come to the Lord in prayer. To focus our desire and will in the direction of relationship with God is something that heaven must surely recognize as the mark of mature humanity.

Such an expression of spiritual maturity is what God encourages in Psalm 32—that, from our own volition, we would choose to remain in relationship with Him. The Lord promises much to those who orient their lives God-ward. With the eagerness of a loving parent, He tells us,

> I will instruct you and teach you in the way you should go;
> I will counsel you with my loving eye on you. (Ps. 32:8)

God's hope is that we would not only desire such a relationship, but would also position our lives in such a way as to receive it daily. We can presume however that the Lord is more used to the opposite from His children. For many of us, it is not until we are in crisis or have a deep need in our lives that we seek God in this way. It is no wonder that, from heaven's perspective, we seem more like a horse or mule which has to be nudged and coerced by "bit and bridle" before we will come to Him.

The Lord equates such a posture with those who "have no understanding" (v. 9). They are dull and unresponsive to the subtleties of His loving invitation. They do not willingly seek God's guidance so the Lord has to lead them instead "by bit and bridle."

"Do not be like this," says the Lord. He appeals to our understanding as He holds out the promise of a gentle relationship that He will never force upon us. Instead God woos us to choose it for ourselves—to come to Him out of the motivation of love, rather than coerced by "bit and bridle."

The personality of prayer is the supreme flower of our humanity, and it is personality with this function that God seeks above all to rear.

P.T. Forsyth

61

So you also, when you have done everything you were told to do, should say, "We are unworthy servants; we have only done our duty."

Luke 17:10

O f all the unruly tendencies of the flesh, spiritual pride is by far the most deceptive. It always feels somewhat more warranted than it should be. You are doing well in your spiritual disciplines. You are finding many ways to serve God in your day. Others are appreciating the encouragement you bring to them. A little self-satisfaction surely seems appropriate. More than any other sin, this one seems so easy to justify.

In her book, *To Believe in Jesus*, Ruth Burrows exposes this sin of spiritual pride as it applies to the things we do for God saying, "Over and over again we must realize how, in what we think of as our love and service of God, lurks a ravenous self-seeking which would use God to inflate self." She adds,

A great deal of what we call charity towards others may actually be self-love, satisfying a need in myself rather than pure seeking of my neighbor's good. The motivation for charity could just as easily be a need to be useful and important, or perhaps a way of alleviating our guilt or of managing the impression of others.

Spiritual pride easily disguises itself as virtue. That is why we so often justify it. Burrows offers an example of how this sin subtly deceives us into believing we are acting for God when, in truth, it is our own spiritual satisfaction that we are serving. She writes,

A priest might have devoted himself to work for the poor. Everyone praises him for his selfless dedication – nothing is too much trouble, nothing too irksome. Then perhaps he is asked to take charge of a well-to-do, stick-in-the-mud parish, and he objects. The reasons brought forward will sound edifying because he must convince himself that he is a man of God, but the real reason is that to work in such a parish will rob him of his sense of doing something worthwhile, something heroic; it would be a spiritual come-down and would tarnish his image of himself. And yet it may be precisely in the non-glamorous situation of an ordinary middle-class atmosphere that the greatest generosity is called for, but it probably won't feel very spiritual.

To feel "spiritual" is the most cherished possession of the devout. But it is a treasure that we must let go of. Our Lord taught us to be careful to not display our good works for the admiration of others (Mat. 6:1, 5), but we must not display them to ourselves either. Paul understood this when he wrote,

> For His sake I have suffered the loss of all things and count them as refuse, in order that I may gain Christ and be found in Him not having a righteousness of my own, based on law, but that which is through faith in Christ (Phil 4: 8-9).

Any form of self-congratulation is ground for spiritual pride. It easily masks what Paul calls a "righteousness of my own"—a spirituality of glory that flatters human pride under the guise of serving God. In the midst of such deception the only safe posture we can assume is that of the servants who, at the end of their day's work, are quick to remind themselves that, "We are unworthy servants; we have only done our duty." Anything more than this we should consider suspect.

62

Jesus welcomed them and spoke to them about the kingdom of God, and healed those who needed healing.

Luke 9:11

People live for many years with what might be called "open wounds." Open wounds are places where we feel stuck by the memory of a particular pain. These memories, still active in our hearts, trigger fears in us that such injuries will reoccur. Even minor wounds in life can result in unresolved stresses that end up determining, much more than we realize, the way we respond to the world and to others.

Open wounds prevent us from fully embracing freedom. They act like a tether that keep us from moving forward. We feel apprehensive about life and less hopeful about the future because our unresolved pains are always suggesting to our imagination the threat of imminent danger.

If this description of an "open wound" resonates in your life, there is a prayer for healing based on the Ignatian prayer of Examen that might be helpful for deepening your dialogue with Jesus in these areas. Here are some steps to lead you in this prayer of Examen.

- Begin your prayer by first placing yourself in the loving presence of God. Here you are reminded that you have always been loved and that, even in the realization that an "open wound" exists in you, there is a potential gift from God that will help you grow in your faith if you are willing to accept it. You may need the Lord's help before you are able to fully accept these difficult experiences as gifts from God. Allow whatever time is necessary to "negotiate" this first crossroads of grace.

- Ask next for the courage to "take up your cross" in order to accept this experience of life as the very place where you might seek and find the Lord.

- Ask Jesus to meet with you there for it is likely that you have long excluded Him from this area of your life, or assumed He is more distant from your wound than He actually is. In prayer ask instead for a new relationship to this narrative—to see your wound as something that Jesus is fully aware of and that He cares deeply about.

- Ask next for a deeper understanding of what the Lord might wish to show you—not only for insight but also for the ability to embrace whatever God reveals to you. Are you prepared to accept your "open wound" as part of the truth of who you presently are? Speak honestly with Jesus about what you are feeling as you revisit this wound.

- Because you are no longer trying to manage your wound—to heal or protect yourself—you are now more prepared to let Jesus minister to you. Allow the Holy Spirit to guide you in this process, following wherever He might lead you and stopping wherever He would have you note something particular regarding this wound. Let God gently untangle the tight knots of your painful history. Spiritual healing is a slow and subtle process. It takes time for this type of prayer to evolve naturally.

• Whenever the Lord shines His light on a particular event related to your "open wound" do not overly analyze it, nor jump too quickly to a solution. You should simply pay attention to your feelings, acknowledging and bringing these insights into your dialogue with Jesus. Ask the Lord to show how faith can be applied to this otherwise fearful memory.

• When you have finished your prayer ask Jesus to sustain the hope you have regarding this process, and to protect you from the despair you might otherwise feel around this topic. Be willing and resolved to return again to this dialogue as often as the Lord requires.

The healing of our "open wounds" is a slow and deliberate work. A sustained faith will help us remain in the hands of the Physician long enough for a relationship of healing to take place. We must learn to approach our open wound less as a problem to be solved and more as a place of dialogue with Jesus about the truth of who we are and who we are becoming. As we enter these places with an open posture we will be led to a more genuine encounter with grace. Gratitude for the God who works out His salvation in our lives will eventually replace the hopelessness of our wounds.

63

Go and sit down in the lowest place, so that when your host comes, he may say to you, "Friend, move up higher."...For all who exalt themselves will be humbled, and those who humble themselves will be exalted.

Luke 14:10-11

People everywhere are trying to find their "seat" in life, often jostling one another for best position. We have all been conditioned to appreciate the importance of reaching for the top. It is natural then for us to strive for advancement and for the upper seats which are, of course, the most coveted ones. In this parable however Jesus tells us to go for the lowest seat, which is actually the easiest one to claim. There is no competition for that one. No one wants it.

"Go and take the lower seat," Jesus tells us, "and wait there until the host comes and says to you, 'Friend, move up higher.'" Jesus calls us to exercise radical faith regarding God's initiatives in our lives—that if we humble ourselves, He will lift us up. But do we really trust Him in this—that the Lord is really that attentive to where you are seated in life? How confident are you that the "Host" will actually notice you in the lowest place, and that He will take the initiative to move you up? Or will others automatically get the better seats and leave you behind?

Such an exercise of faith certainly represents a risky approach to life. If it isn't true then I am foolishly jeopardizing my chances for advancement. The Lord's word challenges the "way that seems right unto man." Should I position myself better for that promotion? Should I draw attention to my qualities so that people will have a better opinion of me? Should I hide my weakness from others lest I lose ground in the eyes of those I want to impress? Such is the anxious disposition that Jesus counters in this parable. Can we trust the Lord enough to wait for Him to lift us up? Or will we anxiously try to manipulate our situation in order to advance ourselves? Jesus' counsel is clear. He tells us to exercise faith and patience as we await His invitation to a better seat.

We often hear the non-Biblical saying that "The Lord helps those who help themselves." But Jesus turns this popular proverb on its head. He is basically saying "The Lord helps those who *don't* help themselves." Shocking isn't it? Consider the quality of faith that not only believes, but dares to act on the principle that if we "humble ourselves in the sight of God, He will lift us up." Can we risk such faith? Can we trust that God will not forget us in the back eddies of life? That our Host will recognize that it is because we have believed Jesus' word that we have chosen the lowest seat? Such is the faith the Lord calls us to, and that He so unambiguously promises to reward. And His greatest reward will be to free us from its alternative—the anxiety that will otherwise motivate us to fend for ourselves.

64

Then he said to them all: "Whoever wants to be my disciple must deny themselves and take up their cross daily and follow me.

Luke 9:23

I've always found it a bit odd when someone facing a hard choice or a difficulty in life says "I'll just give it to the Lord." Is this really what Jesus invites us to do? There are certainly times when it is a necessary corrective, especially when we start assuming that the burdens of life are ours alone to carry. But there is also something suspect in this statement. It seems to shirk the very responsibility that Jesus implies is ours—to carry each day the cross of our life. I think a more subtle relationship is called for here— more of a sharing of life than dumping our difficulties on Jesus.

This balance is beautifully depicted at the Tao Fong Shan facility in Hong Kong where I once led a prayer retreat. There is a small, stone chapel there called the Lotus Crypt. It is a 10' X 12' domed room with only one window and two benches along the side walls. In front of the window there is a small cross on a ledge. And above the cross, in Chinese script, are the words, "Lay down your heavy burden." The invitation from Matt. 11 is clear. Whenever we feel heavy-laden and weighed down by life we can find rest for our souls in Jesus. Meditating on the cross reminds us that Christ bears our sins and that He accompanies us in all our trials.

But there is another sign above the doorway by which we leave this chapel that stresses another truth—the fact that laying our burden with Jesus is an invitation to share the weight of life, not get rid of it. As you leave the chapel this other sign tells you to now "Pick up your cross." Having been fortified by the nearness of Jesus' love, we now return to our active life— even the difficult parts of it—knowing that Christ identifies deeply with the crosses that we too must carry. We are assured that we don't have to carry these crosses alone. Jesus shoulders them with us.

Chinese thinking often juxtaposes opposite statements in order to communicate truth more fully. These two texts provide such a juxtaposition—a balancing of truth where the invitation to "lay down your heavy burden" is not necessarily at odds with Jesus telling us that we also have to carry our cross.

God shares every fear, every struggle and every pain we experience. We are never alone in life. This is the good news of Jesus, who not only identifies with us in the crosses we bear, but also offers Himself as an example in how He carries His own. The two signs in the Lotus Crypt invite us to welcome the yoke of Christ whenever we feel weighed down by life, and then to remain yoked with Him as we negotiate the burden of our days.

65

A bruised reed he will not break, and a smoldering wick he will not snuff out.

Matt. 12:20

Music has always been a natural love for me. No one in my family is musical but somehow, even as a child, I always gravitated to its attraction. I found it easy to teach myself melodies on any instrument I could lay my hands on. I come from a blue-collar town where no one ever took music lessons and it wasn't until I enrolled in a Bachelor of Music program at university that I realized that all of the other students had been taking private lessons for years. In other words, my approach to this vocation, though natural, was quite unorthodox.

I mention this as background as I believe it provides a good example of the type of relationship that can exist between spiritual desire and discipline. In my experience it has always been desire that has led to discipline more than the other way around. No one ever had to tell me to practice music. The desire to do so came naturally from the love I felt for this art. So did the increasing discipline it inspired. My desire to grow as a musician and to perfect this art soon highlighted my limitations related to technique, speed and accuracy. But I never approached the practice of scales or arpeggios—standard fare for anyone taking lessons—as discipline. It came more from my desire to simply push the envelope that was constraining me from being more fluid on my instrument.

I believe our motivation for prayer can benefit from a similar approach. Many people I meet with feel disappointed about their lack of spiritual discipline. They are discouraged at the prospect of trying and failing once more to cultivate a more disciplined prayer life. To someone who comes to me in such despair I usually try to change the focus of their attention from discipline to desire. The issue, as I see it, is not so much one of discipline but more one of desire—their desire for God is simply not strong enough to inspire their discipline.

If we truly desire God, prayer will naturally follow. But if our desire for God is low, discipline, by itself, will never be enough. We are best instead to simply confess our present poverty of spirit and ask the Holy Spirit to restore our first love. In other words, the very poverty we experience can become the subject of our prayer as we say to God, "It is evident Lord that I don't desire you as I wish I did. I want to want you more. Can You help me?"

Such an approach moves us beyond the self-recrimination that so often comes from the false assumption that if only we were more self-disciplined we would have a deeper devotional life. Instead it makes us more dependent on God, who alone can heal the lack of vitality in our hearts and inflame them with spiritual ardour. It is He, after all, who gives us the desires of our hearts (Ps. 37:4).

Jesus assures us that He will not snuff out a smouldering wick. He will help you instead to kindle the flame of your desire so that you will once again be motivated towards God by the Holy Spirit. Your spiritual disciplines will then follow naturally, fueled by the passion of your increasing love and desire for God.

66

"As for me, if I am bereaved, I am bereaved".

Gen. 43:23

Joseph is sold to slave traders by his brothers. But by the grace of God, he becomes the chief administrator of Egypt at a time when there is a great famine in the land. Because of Joseph's foresight, Egypt is the only nation that has a stockpile of grain which it now feeds itself on, as well as sells to foreigners. Joseph's father Jacob sends Joseph's brothers to buy grain from the chief administrator, not realizing that this is the very brother they sold to slavery years ago. During their interview with Joseph they mention they have another brother, Benjamin, a favourite son of Jacob's because he especially loved his mother Rachel, who was also Joseph's mother. The brothers are given grain but Joseph tells them they will not see his face again unless they bring Benjamin with them.

The famine is severe throughout the region and Gen. 43:2 tells us that "when they had eaten all the grain they had brought from Egypt, their father said to them, 'Go back and buy us a little more food.'" The sons remind Jacob that the condition of their return is to bring their brother Benjamin with them which Jacob is reluctant to do, having presumably already lost his son Joseph.

After much deliberation, the patriarch resigns himself to the potential loss of his other beloved son saying "if I am bereaved, I am bereaved." He is in a precarious position. His fate rests in the hands of another and he has no choice but to place himself at the mercy of this narrative.

It is a position we often find ourselves in as well—times when we must totally trust God in situations that could easily work against our favour. Like Jacob, we recognize that the outcome is totally in God's hands. And in the acknowledgement of that truth we somehow find faith to accept the notion that "if I lose, I lose."

Such faith has many applications in life. Perhaps it is the fear of rejection where, as you approach your vulnerable moment, you must be reconciled that, "If they reject me, they reject me." Or perhaps it is the fear of perfectionism that must be countered by the courage to say, "If I fail, I fail." Or maybe it is death itself that you must inevitably approach saying "if I die, I die." We hear something of this disposition in Queen Esther who, feeling trepidation in having to ask the king's mercy for her people, bravely accepts that, "If I perish, I perish." (Esther 4:16)

Such statements might seem more like resignation or fatalism than faith, but there is great wisdom in this disposition. Our prior acceptance of the worst case scenario allows us to move forward according to a more pure faith in God, rather than one restricted only to our hopes. It asserts faith regardless of consequences. "If I fail, I fail." "If they fire me, they fire me." "If they don't like me, they don't like me." "If I suffer loss, I suffer loss." These are all empowering statements that help us move forward as we accept the uncertain outcome of situations we have no control over.

As we embrace the unknowns of our circumstances, and the very real possibility of a worst-case scenario, we disarm the enemy of his greatest weapon against us—our own fear of undesired outcomes. We are then left with a more pure faith that now trusts God even in those precarious situations of life where things can truly go either way. No longer paralyzed by the fear of failure or of harm, we throw ourselves into God's hands, trusting that His mercy will continue to be with us even if the outcome is not as we had hoped.

67

My heart says of you, "Seek his face!"
Your face, Lord, I will seek.

Psalm 27:8

There is nothing more satisfying than to actually do what we most profoundly desire to do. As obvious as this statement sounds, it is surprising how few of us ever get to enjoy that satisfaction, especially as it applies to the spiritual life we desire for ourselves. Instead, we spend far too long in an in-between state of soul, where we know what we want, but can't find the will to do it.

There is a restless desire in each of our hearts that is perhaps best expressed by this verse in Psalm 27, "My heart says of you, 'Seek His face.'" We might not name it as such but at the deepest level of our being, we are all looking for a particular relationship with our Creator—a relationship that satisfies our profound longings for a sense of home, of belonging and of love. To "seek His face" is to pursue this quality of intimacy and nearness with the Living God.

To seek God's face is also how we follow our inevitable destiny. It is being obedient to the most natural prompting of the Spirit in our hearts. In other words, to respond to this urge is to stand in agreement with who we fundamentally are. It is how we participate with our deepest desire and with the ultimate vocation of our souls.

We yearn for a more constant relationship with the living God. And until that relationship is established, we inevitably experience restlessness. How we respond or not to that restlessness is what then determines the shape or shapelessness of our spiritual lives. We either move in response to this yearning, or else we ignore it and remain as we are—often as dissatisfied Christians who have resigned themselves to a much lesser state of soul than is necessary.

The Holy Spirit reminds us often of our profound desire for God. But it takes time for the will to catch up with the heart. To actually do something about this desire is the response of maturity that Psalm 27 is referring to.

My heart says of you "Seek His face." The Psalmist recognizes the groaning in his spirit as a cry to seek God's face. And he is prepared to act on that prompting. *Your face, O Lord, I will seek.* He names the longing in his heart, and then resolves to do the very thing his heart desires him to do. The circle is now complete, as it can be for us as well.

68

Therefore let us move away from the elementary teachings…and let us be taken to maturity.

Heb. 6:1

I was teaching on this passage recently to a Chinese congregation and drawing attention to the verb tense that indicates maturity as something we should "let ourselves be taken to." We were discussing the passive posture of receiving the work of Christ, through submission to the Holy Spirit. After the session someone pointed out to me how the Chinese Bible translates this text to say that we are to "press on to maturity." It struck me what a difference to our understanding the translation of a single word can make.

Whose onus is it to lead us to maturity? Is it ours or God's? Is it work that we assume for ourselves as we "press on" in relationship to this goal? Or is it something we let ourselves be taken to as God leads us to a maturity that only He knows is possible for us?

The Greek verb in question here is *pherometha*. The root of this verb is *phero* which, on its own, means "to carry something." But *pherometha* is the passive, subjunctive tense of that verb which is more accurately translated as "to be carried," or "borne along," as by the current of a stream. We see this verb in Acts 27:15 where Luke, speaking of Paul's misfortune at sea, says, "we allowed ourselves to drift along." Luke uses the same verb in Acts 27:17 where he writes, "they let the ship be driven along." *Pherometha* can also apply to being moved in mind and spirit, as when Peter speaks of godly men who, "being carried along" by the Holy Spirit, spoke from God (2Pet. 1:21).

Our disposition then with regards to maturing is best understood as one of being "carried along." But we do prefer a more active role in the spiritual life, which might be why this slight shift in translation, from the passive to the active tense, occurs not only in the Chinese Bible, but also in many other English translations. Some use the active tense of "let us go on to maturity" (NLT, ESV, KJV), while others insist on the very active sense of "let us press on to maturity" (ASV, NASV).

The NIV however renders this verb as "let us be taken forward to maturity." So does the International Standard Version which has "let us continue to be carried along to maturity." As Dr. David Alan Black, one of the translators of the International Standard Version writes,

> Here the word *pherometha* appears in the passive voice and pictures the Christian as "continually being carried along" to maturity. There is nothing here of "going on," or of "pressing on," or of self-effort, or of struggling to make progress in the Christian life. The author is saying, as it were, "lift your sails and allow yourselves to be borne along to maturity by the Holy Spirit of God." He also uses a tense that implies a process rather than a single act.

Donald Guthrie, in his commentary on the book of Hebrews, writes similarly,

> This second injunction, *go on to maturity*, is expressed in the Greek rather unexpectedly in a passive form, in the sense of 'let us be carried on to maturity (or completeness).' This form suggests an element of yieldedness to a nobler influence.

How we understand our role in relationship to spiritual growth will determine the posture we assume. Will it be by our own efforts, or will we let ourselves be carried on to maturity, like a sailboat borne along by the wind? The latter interpretation better reflects the Greek verb used in this verse. It also seems more in line with the gospel message that emphasizes, in so many ways, that the gift of spiritual life is something that we "freely receive" (Mat. 10:8).

This tendency to lean more towards the active sense of our participation than to the passive posture of receiving our spiritual life from God is something we should all make a note of as it is often the source of much guilt and unnecessary burden. To wait for God's initiative in leading us is not only the better way, it is also the mark of greater maturity. It represents a more refined faith—one that has matured from a form of Christianity that starts with me, to one that begins, more appropriately, with God.

69

Blessed are those whose ways are blameless,
who walk according to the law of the Lord,
Blessed are those who keep his statutes
and seek him with all their heart—
they do no wrong but follow his ways.

Psalm 119:1-3

How daunting it is to think of actually living a fully blameless day. And yet this is just what the Psalmist aspires to in his relationship to God. How does one sustain such a desire in light of the many ways we continue to "do wrong?" And to what extent can we realistically hope to see this spiritual direction unfold in our lives?

I am nowhere near blameless in my day but I do take encouragement from the slow growth that I nevertheless recognize in my own sanctification towards this end. One of the paradoxical ways that sanctity seems to be growing in me is through an increasing sensitivity and awareness of the many ways that I am *not* blameless. Though it used to discourage me, I now find it easier to accept this as the first stage of how God enlists me in the changes needed for my sanctification. The Holy Spirit first convicts me of my sins and then elicits a more urgent desire in me for transformation.

I see this process taking place in all areas of my life but I do notice how God seems to be working mostly from the outside of my life inward. Sanctification happens most evidently or, at least at its first stage, in the outer expressions of my life—in my speech and actions. I think I am more aware today than I used to be when I say or do something wrong. The moment an inappropriate word is on my lips I usually feel regret. And on my better days that sensitivity shows up even before I speak.

I know as well whenever I have behaved wrongly and again, this wisdom helps me be more proactive in avoiding such actions. At the risk of sounding boastful I think I am more blameless in my speech and actions than I used to be. I welcome this and celebrate it as God's good work in me.

But things get more subtle as righteousness goes deeper. What about my thoughts? How blameless am I in how I think throughout a day? I don't seem to be as immediately aware of the unrighteousness that takes place in my mind as I am in my speech and actions. I catch myself much too late ruminating on things I shouldn't be thinking of. And even when I do, I don't seem to have the same control I have over my mouth and actions.

There's a hiddenness about my thought life that works against the motivation to change. Sanctification doesn't seem as urgent here as when the opinions of others, for instance, motivates me to be more blameless in my speech and actions. But again, by God's mercy, I know I am growing in the discomfort I feel over much of what takes place in my thought life. This too gives me hope for sanctification.

And then there is the heart. How blameless am I in where I place my desires? Do I "do no wrong" in the things I choose to exalt in my heart? Do I pursue good desires that lead me to God, or do my desires tend to be more frivolous and self-serving? My heart is deceitful and I don't always recognize the many ways my love is misdirected by my inordinate attachments. But here too I have hope that God is purifying my desires as I see myself being weaned from my superficial wants and needs, and treating as more precious the fleeting gift of God's presence in my life.

And finally there is the will. How pure is my will in the choices I make each day? In what ways do I walk "according to the Lord" rather than "the way that seems right unto me?" Do I submit my will in obedience to God, or do I choose to be free from such constraints? Do I seek the Lord's counsel or do I prefer my own? Grace is slowly teaching me the wisdom of the former over the latter and this too gives me hope.

70

Do you know that all of us who were baptized into Christ Jesus were baptized unto his death? Therefore we have been buried with him by baptism into death so that, just as Christ was raised from the dead by the glory of the Father, so we too might walk in newness of life.

Rom. 6:3-4

I am probably never as freely abandoned to life as at the instant I fall asleep. At that moment I let go of the grip I have on myself and allow myself to be taken to sleep. In a similar way, I expect that the most freedom

I will ever experience on earth will be the moment of my death when I have truly and completely given up all claims to life. Such also is the mystery of our baptism—we are baptized not only into Christ's death but also into our own so that we too might walk in the "newness of life."

Before coming to faith I avoided any form of death that would prevent me from living unto myself. But since faith has graced me, I now find myself much more wary of the forms of life that prevent me from dying unto Christ (e.g. pride, ambition, success, anxiety, fear, inordinate desires, etc.). The Lord has taught me to welcome the loss of such self-rooted concerns. Since we live in the promise of new life, I no longer fear the thought of losing my old life.

"We have been crucified with Christ" (Gal. 2:20). What does that mean other than that we should live as though dead? This might seem a fearful prospect if we are only concerned with the loss of our own life. But, in light of the Resurrection, I know I can confidently risk such dying to myself in full assurance that Christ will raise me anew into a life I would never have known otherwise.

Such is this posture of our baptism, where the symbol of death precedes the new life we are given. It is what Catholics call the "Paschal Mystery." As Dr. Timothy Matovina, a professor at the University of Notre Dame writes,

> The Paschal Mystery is not only a truth about Christ. It is also our spirituality. Dying and rising is the pattern of our life in Christ. We are to imitate Christ's Death and Resurrection by receiving the Spirit of God who makes us more dead to ourselves so that we can live more fully for God in Christ Jesus.

Dying each day to my self, I can now walk according to the true life that, moment to moment, Jesus expresses in me. As I submit my life to Christ, He exalts me with His own. "The finite becomes infinite, the perishable becomes imperishable, what is sown in dishonour is raised in glory and all that is weak in me is raised in power" (1Cor.15:37-44).

A SHORT DISCUSSION I ONCE HAD WITH JESUS

Lord, what does the Paschal Mystery mean? It means dying to your own impulses so that you can be moved by mine.

Lord, how does the Paschal Mystery apply to all the situations of my life? Wait and watch and you will be moved by me.

71

*Enter through the narrow gate. For wide is the gate and
broad is the road that leads to destruction, and many enter
through it. But small is the gate and narrow the road that
leads to life, and only a few find it.*

Matt. 7:13-14

The grace I most often seek in my daily prayer is for Jesus to simply
gather me to His presence—that He would bring my scattered self into
focus and shepherd me to a place of unity with Himself. The idea of being
gathered unto Jesus certainly resonates with the Lord's teaching regarding
the narrow path we are being drawn towards. He invites us to choose for
ourselves this narrow way rather than the wide way we more often prefer.

We usually interpret this passage as primarily evangelistic, where Jesus
is the Way to the Father, and wide is the way of those who refuse Him. But
I believe these verses also apply to how we are to continue living as
Christians in ever-growing proximity to our Lord, which comes from the
narrowing of our focus. Like a river that gets stronger as it passes through
a narrow channel, a more Christ-constrained focus will produce greater
strength in our lives.

A funnel might be another helpful image of the way Jesus shepherds us
towards what is more beneficially narrow in life. Picture the funnel on its
side, with its mouth representing the width and breadth of life, and the
spout being the more narrow way. Where are you today in relationship to
this funnel? Perhaps you are not even in the funnel, but wandering
somewhere outside, not ready yet for the journey inwards. You're in the
general program of Christianity but you know that you are living life with
much more latitude and self-determinacy than you suspect is consistent
with your professed faith.

Growing maturity in faith helps us cooperate with this process of being
shepherded more deeply into the funnel. There is a lessening desire in us for
the wider latitudes we once enjoyed. We also have a better understanding of
how to participate with this process. What are the forces that now encourage
you towards the more narrow way? What people, practices or disciplines help
constrain you as you advance towards this self-simplifying path?

As the Way gets narrower it conforms you more and more in the direction and shape of the funnel spout. It is the funnel that now defines your movements much more than your own self-determination. You find it both restricting and yet freeing as you recognize the hand of God more closely on your life than ever.

More and more your spiritual formation revolves around one simple question: how can I participate more fully with this action of being gathered by Jesus? How can I let myself be shepherded by Him towards the beauty of this narrow relationship? The answer to this question demands only one thing of us—a sustained willingness to let go of our wider agendas in favour of Jesus' promise of a more abundant life.

In our most profound instincts, we all long for such narrowing of our lives—a simplification, a stilling, a silencing of all that spreads us out too thin. To allow Jesus each day to draw us deeper into His "funnel" is to truly live a spiritual life. His promise is that this one choice will lead us, like a river being forced through a narrow chasm, to greater strength and abundance in our lives.

72

If a son asks his father for bread, would he give him a stone instead?

Matt. 7:9

To know God is to trust God. It's as simple as that. And the opposite is just as true. To not trust God is an indicator that we do not really know God. In other words, the "god" we do not trust is not really God, but rather a false imagining of our own making. This reasoning also applies to people who believe, for instance, that God is absent, that He has wronged them, or somehow betrayed or abandoned them. The untrustworthy god that they are imagining is not truly God.

To accept the fact that such "gods" are actually fictitious projections of our own fears is a first step towards establishing a more truthful relationship with the real God. Confessing our false images provides an opportunity for us to start all over again— a chance to be re-introduced to this "Jesus I never knew." The alternative is to continue living in a dysfunctional relationship with the "god" of our fears.

The "God who cannot be trusted" does not really exist. And yet, through our imaginations, we often live in complex relationships with such non-existent gods. It is important to recognize the presence of false idols in our theological thinking. Such caricatures are most readily identified by their un-Godlike character,—e.g. the god who is always angry with you, the god who is always disappointed in you, the god who is always demanding more from you. Or, conversely, the god who doesn't care what you do or how you live.

There are many Christians whose relationship with the spirit they call "God" actually produces desolation in them. But, mercifully, the Lord will not allow us to establish our foundation on such unstable idols. Instead, the inner turmoil these relationships produce is meant to reveal to us the unfittingness of our images of God.

The Lord once taught His disciples how ridiculous it would be to not trust His Father. He asked rhetorically, "if a son asks his father for bread, would he give him a stone instead?" Of course not. That would be laughable. And yet that is exactly what we imply when we imagine God as not being good or faithful towards us.

To know God is to trust God. We can then rest in the secure fact that He is good—in other words, in the truth of who He really is. Faith is what assures us of God's character—that He loves me, that He is merciful, that He is trustworthy, that He is faithful, that He understands me, and that He will never abandon me. To think of Him otherwise, as Jesus suggests, would be laughable.

Those who know you, Lord, will trust you.

Psalm 9:9 (Good News)

73

Without me you can do nothing.

John 15:5

Spiritual growth is actually a very simple matter. According to John 15, we need only remain attached to the vine of Christ and we will automatically bear the fruit of the Spirit. But as Jesus' parable also plainly teaches, this same fruit will also wither in us whenever we leave the vine.

One of the obvious truths that John 15 illustrates is that the virtues of God do not originate or reside in us but in Christ, whose righteousness is "imparted" to us (2 Cor 5:21). Virtue, in other words, is derivative. The fruit of the Spirit is simply the evidence of the Lord's presence as it moves in and out of our lives according to our conformity with His character. To the degree that we are present to Christ, the character of God is present within us. But if we are not attached to the Source of this character, these same virtues automatically wither in us.

Consider your own experience of "withering" as it applies to each fruit of the Spirit that Paul lists in Gal. 5:22-23 (love, joy, peace, forbearance, kindness, goodness, faithfulness, gentleness and self-control). Consider, for instance the fact that whenever you are detached from the Spirit:

- Your love withers. You become more self-oriented, more self-seeking.

- Your joy withers. Your life becomes flat and uninteresting to you.

- Your peace withers. Your heart becomes more restless, anxious and full of turmoil.

- Your forbearance withers. You lose patience and have little room in your heart for others.

- Your kindness withers. You no longer feel inspired to make that extra effort to help others.

- Your goodness withers. You become more aware of your selfishness and lack of charity.

- Your faith withers. You feel more fearful about life. The future seems more worrisome. The past more regretful.

- Your gentleness withers. You have fewer resources to be magnanimous with your circumstances, with others, or with yourself. You find yourself more angry in your responses to life.

- Your self-control withers. Your discipline cannot hold. You end up feeling tepid, lazy and lukewarm. You know that you are not who you could be in this life, but you lack motivation to do anything about it.

If you can relate to any of these conditions, you would be wise to not overly psychologize your experiences of deficiency. Instead, recognize them for what they are—a withering of your spiritual life—and come to God for the restoring of your soul. Such withering requires not better management, but for you to simply return to the vine of Christ. For as Jesus plainly taught us, "without Me, you can do nothing."

74

The light shines in darkness, but the darkness has not understood it.

John 1:5

The coming of Jesus has certainly confused our experience of spirituality. Our relationship to divinity has become much more subtle. Gone are the well-defined boundaries that separated what is godly from what is merely human. Gone is the clear-cut distinction between the sacred and the common. And gone is the obvious logic of heaven and earth as two separate geographies. Instead, we have divinity mingled with humanity, and sanctity somehow shining through the darkness of our sins.

The OT was painstaking in the ways it delineated the gulf between what is divine and what is human. The tabernacle itself was an elaborate object lesson demonstrating, in the most graphic terms, the distance that separates purity from sin. Its main purpose was to communicate the fact that God is holy—and that we are not. The fact that such clear boundaries exist was a given in the OT. But Jesus has changed all that. He who is both human and divine has confused the lines of demarcation that made sense of our lot.

When we knew ourselves uniquely as sinners it was easy to grasp the distance between ourselves and God. But now we're not so sure. Jesus has blurred the lines. He has torn the curtain that not only kept us from God, but also kept God from us. Separating the weeds from the wheat isn't as easy as it was before. Even in our own hearts, it is difficult to discern what is human and what is of the Spirit. For, in the person of Christ, the two have mysteriously become one.

The light shines in darkness. God now co-exists with the most profane aspects of our humanity. He dwells in the midst of our basest instincts. He skirts on the edges of our sins, dances in and around our iniquities. Nothing impedes His grace. Though sin persists in us, divinity is undeterred. Though our depravity is evident, Jesus continues to shepherd us towards a sanctity that somehow by the grace His Holy Spirit already exists within us.

The darkness has not understood this. His glorious Truth beckons from deep within our hearts, a righteousness that we feel called to become. Though we live much of our lives out of sync with this truth, Christ's love relentlessly conforms and aligns us to its movements. Though our inner lives flicker in and out of darkness, His presence continually lights our way.

Such is the mystery of the Incarnation. We cannot understand how or why this Light persists, but we nevertheless grow in the confidence that not even our sins can thwart its purpose. Praise be to God for His steadfast ways! In spite of our confusing darkness, the Light of His unconditional grace is somehow making perfect sense of our lives.

75

The Lord searches every heart and understands every desire and every thought. If you seek him, he will be found by you.
1Chron. 28:9

The grace I usually seek in prayer is that of a silent and still heart in relationship to God's presence. It's the most intimate hope I presently have for my prayer. But I know that the disposition of stillness is not always possible in me. If so, I ask the Lord then to at least lead me to productive thoughts. Both experiences of prayer—discursive and non-discursive—can offer rich opportunities for spiritual growth. For the Lord "understands every desire and every thought."

Through discursive prayer, or meditation, we get to work through the details of our lives with God. We bring our questions to the Lord which often lead to a more precise understanding of ourselves and our spiritual lives. In the light of His truth we get to sift through all the relationships that define our life. We are also more attentive to whatever adjustments God is calling us to make in these.

Many such benefits attest to the good that can come through our mental dialogues with God. But there is another, more beneficial way of prayer that lies beyond meditation. And it is the inevitable fruit of any maturing relationship where words become less and less necessary the more familiar we are with the other person.

There comes a point in discursive prayer when words have served their purpose. In the midst of our active dialogue with God, we start sensing another invitation calling us to a deeper, more instinctive relationship. Our hearts suspect that a greater intimacy with God is possible beyond the limits of mental prayer. We begin exploring a more wordless form of prayer—what the ancients called "the prayer of the heart."

People who are used to praying for longer periods are certainly familiar with this transition that leads from a "prayer of the mind" to a "prayer of the heart." Our growing desire to rest in God starts shifting our focus from the dialogue that is going on in our minds to the more passive form of sighing that takes place in our hearts. The very act of thinking becomes wearying as the subtle energies required to keep a mental dialogue going eventually exhaust us. We respond more readily now to the invitation to pray, as the desert fathers taught, "with the mind descended into the heart."

Loosening the tight grip we have on ourselves we sink into our hearts as we begin exploring a more direct, spirit-to-Spirit communication with God. We find ourselves mysteriously led towards the "quiet waters" that lie just below the surface of our active selves. If only for a few seconds, this cessation of thought produces in us a most welcome relief from the constant churning of data that our hearts are usually subjected to.

No longer distracted by the continuous narrative of thought, the soul now communes with God in a much more direct way. Concepts or imaginings are no longer required as the material for our prayer, for we simply rest now in the sufficiency of God's immediate presence. And in this disposition of stillness and silence we sense that we are communing with the most creative act of life—the moment-to-moment experience of God loving us as we return that same love to Him. We have sought Him and we have found Him. There is nothing more to do now but to simply enjoy each other in the spirit of prayer.

76

*I saw the Lord, high and exalted, seated on a throne; and
the train of his robe filled the temple.....Then I heard the
voice of the Lord saying, 'Whom shall I send? And who will
go for us?' And I said, 'Here am I. Send me!'*

Isa. 6:1, 8

The beauty of God has a way of transforming us. It never leaves us indifferent or unaffected but always moves us towards action, sending us back into the world as witnesses of what we have seen. As Hans Urs von Balthasar puts it, "Beauty works its way into our bones, into the sinews of our life, indelibly marking us, and then setting us off."

Isaiah, having tasted the goodness of the Lord, is sent out as a herald of the beauty he has seen. As the Catholic theologian Robert Barron writes,

> The one who has been grasped by the beautiful is like the woman in the Gospel who breaks open the alabaster jar at the feet of Jesus and allows the aroma of the perfume to fill the entire house; she is willing to break open her life in order to witness to what she has seen and heard.

Experiences of beauty always imply mission. We are changed by what God has shown us. And whatever we receive in such encounters is always for the sake of others. As Barron notes,

> Visions of the divine are never given merely for the sake of private edification or contemplation. The "seeing" is never an end in itself. On the contrary, there is always a commission attached to the insight. Vision opens you to mission. You have been shown so that others might see as well.

Countless examples of this movement from "seeing" to "being sent" are found in Scripture. Moses is so marked by his encounter with God that his face becomes radiant. He doesn't stay on the mountaintop but comes back down to set his people free. Saul of Tarsus, dazzled by Christ's light, is sent to Damascus where he is given a mission to carry the message of Jesus to the gentiles. And Peter, the first to discern that Jesus is the Messiah, is immediately given the commission to anchor and ground the community through which the glory he has recognized will now be proclaimed to the world.

God, it would seem, does not disclose himself without purpose. He commissions the one who has seen with a call for service to the whole community, a call that is both compelling and inescapable. The beauty of the Lord becomes a fire within us, prompting us to a missionary life of proclamation. As Barron puts it, "To refuse this call would be tantamount to refusing the best of oneself. To ignore it would be to ignore the person we are meant to be." He adds,

> The summons from God is like the coal placed on the lips of Isaiah, or the fire burning uncomfortably in the bones of Jeremiah, or the compulsion that Paul feels to proclaim the Gospel: "I am ruined if I do not preach it!" The beauty of God so possesses us that our very identity, our very person, becomes the mission to communicate this to the world.

Whatever we have seen of Christ has transformed us into witnesses of the gospel. And the same mystery that first drew us to His beauty now sends us out to share with the world the glory we have seen.

A BIBLICAL APOLOGETICS
FOR CONTEMPLATIVE
PRAYER

What is Biblical about Contemplative Prayer? It is a fair question that any responsible Christian should be prepared to answer. I would like to offer the following Scriptural apologetics for the God-initiated life of contemplative prayer and for the spiritual direction that such prayer implies. May these meditations help secure our confidence that we are truly pursuing Jesus' intent for us, according to Scripture.

PART 1: SEEKING GOD'S FACE

Contemplative prayer is simply an extension, or natural evolution of all prayer. It is a prayer posture that explores the more receptive side of our relationship with God. As such it is not necessarily another form of prayer but one that more intentionally anticipates and prepares itself for God's initiative. Contemplative prayer traces the deep desires of the heart that lead to God as the ultimate object of our longing. It is the response of our hearts to the invitation we hear throughout Scripture to "seek God's face." (1Ch 16:11, 2Ch 7:14, Ps, 24:6, Hos. 5:15) David describes something of the profound longing of love that inspires contemplative prayer when he writes, "My heart says of you, "Seek his face!" Your face, LORD, I will seek" (Ps. 27:8). Such prayer awakens in us the desire to seek not only the knowledge of God, but a growing intimacy with the person of Christ (Jn 5:39).

A. W. Tozer once spoke of the curious logic whereby Christians assume that "once they have found God, they no longer need to seek Him." And yet to seek intimacy with God is the very reason for which we were given life. As Paul explains to the Athenians,

From one man God made every nation, that they should inhabit the whole earth; and He determined the times set for them and the exact places where they should live. God did this so that we would seek Him and perhaps reach out for Him and find Him, though He is not far from each one of us. (Acts 17:26-28)

Not only does the Lord encourage such seeking, He also delights in our response. As the book of Proverbs declares, "I love those who love me, and those who seek me find me" (Prov. 8:17). Other Scriptures, as well, gives us assurance that if we seek God we will surely find Him (Dt. 4:29, Jer. 29:13). Jesus Himself invites us to prioritize this quest (Mt. 7:7) and affirms His friend Mary who chooses intimacy with Him over the distracting busyness of life. What Jesus says to her He says to us as well, "only one thing is needed. Mary has chosen what is better" (Lk. 10:42).

Seeking God then is an intentional form of prayer whereby we exalt our relationship with God over all other relationships that define our lives. Such seeking inevitably implies the conversion of our wills, as well as the purifying of our desires as we choose, in all areas of life, to exchange our self-orientation for the precious pearl of new life in Christ (Mt. 13:45).

To seek and find God's face then is our chief vocation. It is our glory. As the book of Proverbs states, "it is the glory of God to conceal a matter; to search out a matter is the glory of kings (and queens)" (Prov. 25:2). How many people, in seeking God have become wise, more humble and more free?

Because of the many veils that remain over our hearts God seems more hidden to us than He really is. But as our hearts are increasingly unveiled, our own glory as Abba's children is revealed as we more perfectly reflect God's image (2Cor. 3:16). This is the relationship of intimate love and closeness that God most desires with us. From the mysterious place of His seeming absence the Lord bids us to come near saying, "Who is he who will devote himself to be close to me?" (Jer. 30:21). The Book of James also assures us that, as we draw near to God, He will also draw near to us (Jam. 4:8).

Contemplation, then, is a form of prayer that intentionally cultivates the discipline of seeking and finding God. It takes place in an environment of minimal distraction where the heart is most free to discover and respond to its profound longing for unity with God. The desire to seek the Lord's "face," as well as the ongoing conversion of our hearts in purifying this desire, are what inspire the practice of Christian contemplative prayer.

It is this motivation as well as the particular objectives of contemplative prayer that make it different in intent from other types of prayer that we are also called to practice—notably prayers of intercession and petition. It represents spiritual growth in the area of increasing given-ness to God (Rom. 12:1). In this it has much in common with the disposition of prayer that most defined Jesus' life—He who "made Himself nothing" (Phil. 2:7) in order to remain perfectly united with His Father.

PART 2: SEEKING LOVE

Contemplative prayer represents the natural progression of love towards greater intimacy with God. As John of the Cross taught, "it is the nature of love to desire unity with the object of its love." This is why Scripture so often uses the image of marriage as the most appropriate metaphor for the love relationship that God desires with us (Hos. 1-3, Isa. 54:5, Eph. 5:31-32, Rev. 19:7). From the deep yearning that such prayer evokes, our own hearts cry out as well for unity with our "Abba" (Gal. 4:6) What we seek is nothing short of the intimacy of marital hope whereby "the two shall become one." (Mark 10:8)

Contemplative prayer then is a receptive posture that submits, in love, to the advances of God. It is an expression of utter trust such as David describes in Psalm 131 whereby he "stills and quiets his soul" in order to rest more fully in the embrace of God. This "resting in love" also represents our most basic sense of "home." It anticipates the spiritual rest that the writer of Hebrews encourages when he writes,

> There remains then, a Sabbath-rest for the people of God; for anyone who enters God's rest also rests from his own work, just as God did from his. Let us, therefore, make every effort to enter that rest. (Heb. 4:9-10)

To rest from our own "work" in prayer expresses faith that the Holy Spirit is truly active in this relationship. And from this place of stillness, we come to a more precise knowledge and experience of the Spirit's movements within us. In the immediacy of our experience, we come to know, that "He is Lord" (Ps. 46:10).

Over and over, the Psalms speak of our deep longing for intimacy with God, often equating it with the essential needs of the body for food or water (Ps. 42:1-2, Mat. 5:6). It is a longing that grows in intensity the more we taste that the Lord is good. Psalm 84, for instance, celebrates the passion of love when it speaks of the heart and flesh crying out for God, and of the soul yearning, even fainting, for the courts of the Lord (Ps. 84:2). Receptive prayer heightens and concentrates these deep longings for unity with God. To seek the fruit of contemplative prayer then is an expression of our desire to be more consistently open and available to God. In this, contemplative prayer is simply a response to Jesus' command to "remain in His love" (Jn 15:9).

As our experience of God's love grows, so does our resolve to never leave again. Like Ulysses lashing himself to the mast of his ship so that he would not be lured to the shore by the Sirens, we too seek to position ourselves as close as possible to the Fount from which we draw our life. Like the branch that remains fruitful in the vine (Jn 15:5), we learn to "remain in His love" through the disposition that contemplative prayer teaches.

PART 3: SEEKING GOD'S WILL

Contemplative prayer is one of the ways we respond to the Spirit's invitation to surrender more fully to God, in whom we live, move and have our being (Acts 17:28). It is the life that Jesus envisioned for us when He prayed to His Father, "May they be one with us, just as you and I are one" (Jn 17:21) For Jesus, the pronoun "I" was always understood as "We." He did not suffer the illusions of autonomy and of separation as we do.

Our Lord's deepest desire is that we too should live according to the same relationship of loving obedience that He enjoys with the Father—a life lived in the immediacy of God's will (Jn 5:19, 12:49-50). Contemplative prayer, then, seeks to live more in tandem with the conformity that Christ modeled for us (Rom 8:29). As we grow in this disposition, our desires become more congruent with the Father's will in all that we are and do.

Through the prophet Jeremiah, the Lord anticipates the gift of the Holy Spirit at Pentecost by which He imparts to us the immediacy of His will. Referring to this gift as the "new covenant" He says, "I will put my law in their minds and write it on their hearts" (Jer. 31:33). The prophet Ezekiel also speaks of this initiative from God when he writes,

> I will give you a new heart and put a new spirit in you; I will remove from you your heart of stone and give you a heart of flesh. And I will put my Spirit in you and move you to follow my decrees and be careful to keep my laws. (Eze. 36:26-27)

Again, a similar conversion of the heart is echoed in Eze. 11:19 when the Lord says,

> I will give them an undivided heart and put a new spirit in them; I will remove from them their heart of stone and give them a heart of flesh. Then they will follow my decrees and be careful to keep my laws.

In contrast to our hearts of stone, which are insensitive to the movements of God, the heart of flesh represents conversion towards a life that is more attentive to the Lord's promptings. As we submit to these movements, we reflect more accurately the particular image of God that each of us is meant to be (2Cor. 3:18). Contemplative prayer then is the crucible in which we place ourselves for the conversion of our hearts towards greater conformity with God's creativity in our lives.

God's will, now imparted to us directly, is no longer a set of marching orders that comes from outside us, but more a movement of the Spirit, written on our hearts, that we are to follow out of a growing love for He who moves us. Though it conforms perfectly to Scripture, the onus of our obedience has shifted from adherence to the external and prescribed laws to that of a growing sensitivity and submission to the immediate promptings of God's life within us. It requires not so much the discipline of self-will, leading to obedience, as the loving and continual submission of the self to its Creator. It is God Himself who promises to move our hearts in accordance with His will—to place in us the desire to obey all that He is doing in and through us.

The apostle Paul as well speaks of a movement of Spirit that takes place within us in accordance with the will of God. In his letter to the Romans, he writes of the prayer that is active in our hearts as a result of the Holy Spirit's presence within us.

> The Spirit helps us in our weakness; for we do not know how to pray as we ought, but that very Spirit intercedes with sighs too deep for words. And God, who searches the heart, knows what is the mind of the Spirit, because the Spirit intercedes for the saints according to the will of God. (Rom 8:26-27 RSV)

Such is the God-breathed prayer that contemplative prayer attends to. It surrenders to the initiative of the Spirit, exchanging the self-willed life for one that more fittingly has its origins in God. As Jesus tells Nicodemus, in order to partake in the kingdom of heaven we must be born "from above," (i.e. according to the immediate will of our Creator), rather than "from below" (i.e. according to our own best intentions) (Jn 3:6, Jn 1:12-13).

Through contemplative prayer we sacrifice our autonomy on the altar of God's will (Rom. 12:1). As the clay submits to the Potter, so we allow ourselves to be refashioned according to the higher ways of God (Jer. 18:4). No longer drinking from our own cisterns, we draw life instead from the living water of Christ (Jer. 2:13). Such is the trusting disposition of love and submission that contemplative prayer fosters in us.

PART 4: SEEKING A MORE CHRIST-LIKE HUMILITY

Contemplative prayer humbles us and makes us more disposed to yield our lives to God. It is a posture of self-offering through which we imitate the humility of Christ who perfected His own obedience (Heb. 5:8) to the Father's will by making Himself nothing (Phil. 2:7). Growing in our dependence on God, we come to trust and anticipate the goodness of His ways rather than following those of our own understanding, or of our best intentions (Prov. 3:5-6).

Such prayer invites us to increasingly surrender ourselves, out of love, to whatever God is calling us to be. It is the posture of the clay that trusts the Potter's hand without having to second-guess God's purposes (Isa. 45:9). It is the disposition that God affirms in Mary when she offers herself unequivocally to the Lord's initiative saying, "Let it be unto me, according to Your word" (Luke 1:38). And it is the union that Jesus encourages when He invites us to exchange the heavy burden of our autonomous life for His much lighter yoke (Mt. 11:30).

Contemplative prayer seeks humble obedience to the Divine will that is always acting upon us. As the apostle Peter teaches us, God has given "his very great and precious promises, so that through them we may participate in the divine nature" (2Pet. 1:4). As we defer to God's initiative in our lives, our hearts align more closely with the Spirit whose very purpose is to call us to conformity with Christ (Rom 8:29).

Paul too exhorts us to seek the more immediate will of God in our lives saying, "since we live by the Spirit, let us keep in step with the Spirit" (Gal. 5:25). It implies a growing attentiveness to the Spirit's movement—the very fruit that contemplative prayer fosters in us. Such prayer encourages the humility of silence and stillness. We learn to rest from our own works (Heb. 4:10) in order to be more attentive, and obedient, to God's initiative.

To seek the Lord's preference for our lives is also what Paul encourages when he tells us to "find out what pleases the Lord" (Eph. 5:10). We welcome as our own whatever God's desire for us might be. Such was the disposition that Jesus modeled for us throughout His life, most notably in the garden of Gethsemane (Mat. 26:39). It requires the same humble disposition by which John the Baptist recognized that "He (Christ) must increase and I must decrease (Jn. 3:30)."

Jesus taught on many occasions that, in order to find our lives, we must first lose them (Matt.10:39). Paul, as well, teaches that it is only to the degree that we have died to ourselves that Christ's resurrection can become the Source of our new life (Rom. 6:4). Presenting himself as an example of this new creation, the apostle proclaims that, "the life I live is not my own, it is Christ who lives in me" (Gal. 2:20). He has exchanged the old man for the new (Col. 3:9-10).

Contemplative prayer then is our response to the Spirit's invitation to live more humbly in tandem with God's will. It fosters growth not only in our attentiveness to the movements of the Holy Spirit, but also in our trust of God and of His mysterious ways as the ongoing Creator of our lives. Jesus alludes to the humility that such prayer will require of us when He says, "Unless you change and become like little children you will never enter the kingdom of heaven" (Matt.18:3).

From the increasing state of given-ness that contemplative prayer encourages—a life more yoked with the humility of Jesus—we come to enjoy a foretaste of the "glorious freedom of the children of God" (Rom. 8:21). For as Paul writes elsewhere, "where the Spirit of the Lord is, there is freedom" (2Cor. 3:17). Jesus' yoke is easy and His burden is truly light. This is what we discover as we "let the peace of Christ rule in our hearts" (Col. 3:15). Only then can we bear authentic witness to the truth of Paul's words that "the mind controlled by the Spirit is peace and life." (Rom. 8:6)

ABOUT IMAGO DEI

1

Blessed are those you choose and bring near to live in your courts! We are filled with the good things of your house, of your holy temple.

Psalm 65:4

I've never been more passionate, more focused, happier, more creative, inspired or efficient in all my life as I am now. And I know, without a doubt, that there is one simple reason for this—I have never been more consistently prayerful in my life. There is a direct relationship between the discipline of daily prayer that God's grace has sustained in me these many years, and the amazing transformation I have experienced in all aspects of my life and ministry.

When I consider the particular graces that foster the discipline of contemplative prayer in my life I am fully aware of the people, structures, and practices that God uses to focus me in my spiritual direction. In this, I am especially appreciative of what I receive from the ministry of Imago Dei. It is a precious gift to my life and I am grateful for the spiritual fruit it encourages in me.

From the very beginning, this ministry has been a catalyst for the encouragement of spiritual growth and transformation in those who desire this in their lives. We've created resources, weekly meditations, taught seminars, led retreats and fostered a network of small groups that meet regularly for the simple purpose of encouraging a sustained response to God. Our discussions, our contemplative prayer and worship, and our weekly celebration of Communion provide many opportunities for the Holy Spirit to breathe upon us and to remind us of the varied ways that "deep calls to deep" within us.

An essential spiritual conversation has begun among us about things we never get to talk about at church, and it has proven to be a profound basis for fellowship, mutual encouragement and effective growth in our spiritual lives. Our desire for God is quickened and our vision for spiritual community becomes more focused as we dialogue honestly with each other about matters of the soul. We are learning how to articulate our shared experience of the mystery of God's ways.

There are many things that Imago Dei is not. But, for those who long for such encouragement, it has become a true catalyst for spiritual growth and vitality. The fact that there are more and more people who recognize and value this emphasis assures us that we are on the right track.

In the simplicity of what we are learning through this ministry, two things have been particularly impressed by the Holy Spirit: that as we mature in our faith, we must learn how to increasingly submit to God's ways through prayer. And that, in perfecting our obedience, we must become more responsive to, and more reliant on, God's initiative in our lives. May such simple but essential objectives continue to lead us, in the coming years, towards fruitful engagement with the Living Christ.

> *There, in the presence of the LORD your God, you and your*
> *families shall eat and shall rejoice in everything you have put*
> *your hand to, because the LORD your God has blessed you.*

Deut. 12:7

2

> **All by itself the soil produces grain—first the stalk, then the**
> **head, then the full kernel in the head.**

Mark 4:28

The overall objective of Imago Dei's ministry is similar to the old adage that motivates missionaries: "Give a man a fish and you will feed him for a day, but teach him how to fish and you will feed him for life." Our hope is not to establish ourselves as the local fish market, where people come to be fed for a day, but to teach and encourage people to fish on their own—

to seek and find God through prayer so that they can become who they are called to be in this world.

The vocabulary of spiritual direction that we use at Imago Dei resonates deeply with the invitation many people feel God already making to their hearts. They seem appreciative of the language we speak, and the emphasis we share in our discussions. This language allows us to communicate our deepest yearnings for God and the truth we seek in our innermost beings. It both affirms what we believe is possible for the spiritual life, as well as provides the basis for a dialogue that encourages a life of prayer in the context of community.

Though our emphasis is mostly on personal prayer, many people attend Imago Dei groups for weeks, months or even years before ever establishing a regular discipline of prayer for themselves. In the meantime they glean from others who have cultivated such practices in their own lives, and their hearts are kindled in the direction of this hope for themselves.

Through the consistent fanning of their desire for God, people do eventually develop a more disciplined prayer life. They enter the "school of prayer" where the Holy Spirit helps them negotiate the ebbs and flows of the flesh that contest the primacy of God in their lives. Prayer soon becomes a non-negotiable feature of their lives. They recognize it as the hub around which all else revolves, and gladly submit to God's initiatives in their hearts, and in their circumstances. At this point, whether they realize it or not, they have become sources of encouragement and motivation to others who hope to establish a similar priority in their own lives.

An even more significant sign of maturity happens however in people when they begin to look more intentionally outward, encouraging others in this pilgrimage of trust. They pursue personal prayer more diligently now, not only for themselves but for the sake of others. They study and equip themselves through books, retreats or courses in order to better serve the mystery of God's invitation in the lives of others. Some become leaders of Imago Dei groups, facilitating communities of encouragement where this type of nurturing takes place. Others train to become spiritual directors, accompanying people more closely along their pilgrimage. Some who are pastors, convinced of the priority of prayer in their ministry, bring such expressions to the centre of their communities' self-understanding. Prayer becomes the catalyst for the Spirit-birthed churches they are becoming.

Such is the path of growth that we are witnessing in the lives of people around us —first the stalk, then the head, then the full kernel in the head. Jesus said, "You will know a tree by its fruit" (Luke 6:44). The sustained vitality of spiritual life that many are enjoying is proof indeed that God is doing a good work among us, and that it pleases the Lord to bless the fruit this tree bears. For this we give thanks.

SCRIPTURE INDEX

CPSIA information can be obtained
at www.ICGtesting.com
Printed in the USA
BVHW040323030522
635978BV00018B/73